The**5**Money
Personalities™

The 5 Money Personalities™

Speaking the Same Love and Money Language

Scott & Bethany Palmer

THE MONEY COUPLE®

THOMAS NELSON

Since 1798

NASHVILLE   DALLAS   MEXICO CITY   RIO DE JANEIRO

Published in Nashville, Tennessee, by Thomas Nelson. Thomas Nelson is a registered trademark of Thomas Nelson, Inc.

Thomas Nelson, Inc. titles may be purchased in bulk for educational, business, fund-raising, or sales promotional use. For information, please e-mail SpecialMarkets@ThomasNelson.com.

Library of Congress Cataloging-in-Publication Data

Palmer, Scott, 1971–
  The 5 money personalities : speaking the same love and money language / Scott and Bethany Palmer.
    p. cm.
  ISBN 978-0-8499-6478-7 (trade paper)
  1. Couples—Finance, Personal. 2. Finance, Personal. 3. Financial security.
4. Finance, Personal—Religious aspects—Christianity. I. Palmer, Bethany, 1965–
II. Title. III. Title: Five money personalities.
  HG179.P1887 2013
  332.0240086'56—dc23   2012040164

Printed in the United States of America

13 14 15 16 17 QG 5 4 3 2 1

To our sons, Cole and Cade:
We love you both.

Contents

Acknowledgments

We are so thankful for the amazing people God has put into our lives to make this newest book a reality! Thank you to the best sons parents could ever ask for, Cole and Cade. Your flexibility, encouragement, and ability to jump on a plane at any time to spread our message of hope are a gift to us.

Thank you to both of our parents, who have done nothing but support us. Thank you, too, for your examples of hard work and long, strong marriages.

Dan Merrell and John Thompson from Propeller have been a huge blessing. Their input with the brand and direction of The Money Couple has been invaluable. You guys are amazing to work with, and we would not be here without your guidance.

Thank you to Matt Baugher and the amazing team at Thomas Nelson. Thank you for believing in our message and our passion for making marriages better.

Carla Barnhill continues not only to be a great friend, but also her ability to write and shape our message has been such a great blessing over the past five years.

We are also so thankful to the couples who have opened up their Money Relationships to us. They have let us guide, direct, and learn from them.

New Life Church in Colorado Springs has been an incredible support to us along this journey. Thank you, Pastor Brady Boyd, for your friendship and faith in us.

Our goal is to change relationships for the better and make marriages awesome. Praise be to God for all that He can accomplish!

INTRODUCTION

How Ninety Days Can Change Your Life

I have always been an athlete. Scott? Not so much. So early in our marriage, when Scott came home one day and told me he was going to run a marathon, I tried really hard not to laugh out loud. Scott had never run a mile, much less 26.2 of them. As I sat there in silent shock, he explained that he'd found a training program online that would have him trained and ready in ninety days. I was still convinced there was no way he could do this.

That spring, Scott ran the Los Angeles Marathon. Sometimes he still wears his medal around the house. Scott's determination showed me that it's possible to make major changes in your life in just ninety days.

Then something else happened in our lives that convinced us amazing things can happen in just ninety days. In 2008, I was diagnosed with Stage 3 breast cancer. I had gone in for a routine mammogram and didn't think twice about it. About a week later, we were on vacation and I got a message to call my doctor. I called her back and she said, "Are you sitting down?" That's never what you want to hear from your doctor. That's when she told me I had breast cancer.

We let the news sink in as best we could. Because we didn't know all the details of my diagnosis, we decided not to tell our boys about the cancer just yet. We decided to finish out our vacation and deal with this life-changing news when we got home.

We met with the oncologist, and I tried not to lose my mind with the worry, the fear, and the questions that raced around in my head. My treatment path was clear— I'd take a medication that was developed to fight the kind of cancer I had and then go through chemotherapy. We prepared ourselves for the long road ahead and all that it would involve.

Chemo does a number on your body. It kills everything bad—the cancer—but it also kills everything good. And in some ways, chemo killed off not just the cancer but also my spirit. I was as low as a person can get.

But then I started to see a little bit of light at the end of the tunnel. I had ninety days of chemo ahead of me. I thought, *If I can just get through the next ninety days, I can beat this.* And with the help and support from my wonderful family, friends, and Scott, and the strength I found in

God, I got better. Our friends and family carried us during those ninety days, and we made it through the roughest time in our marriage.

Those ninety days changed our lives. And your life can change in ninety days too. As you work through this book, you will see a transformation in your relationship. After ninety days of doing something, it becomes more than a habit; it becomes a lifestyle. We believe you can take a marriage that's struggling, a relationship that's riddled with financial infidelity and mistrust, and turn it around. We believe you can adopt a lifestyle where arguments about money are a thing of the past, a lifestyle where you make decisions out of mutual love and respect.

When Scott was running his marathon, he got to mile 24 and just stopped. He was mentally and emotionally spent. Suddenly a man came running up alongside him and took him by the arm. This man, a total stranger, started talking to Scott, asking him questions about his life, and telling Scott about himself. Before they knew it, they'd reached the finish line.

The journey toward a strong Money Relationship can feel like a long haul, but if you are committed to linking arms and finishing this journey together, you can make it happen. By picking up this book, you have made the decision to strengthen your relationship and dream about the future. It won't happen overnight, and it won't happen without both of you deciding you want to start fresh and build a great life together. But it can happen. We've seen it over and over again. You can make it happen!

(For more information and details about Bethany's journey, go to TheMoneyCouple.com.)

The Big Picture

Before you jump in, we want to be clear about something: this book is not a guide to managing your money. You won't find tricks for creating a balanced budget or tips on saving money. We aren't going to teach you how to find the best investments or how to reduce your mortgage. There are plenty of books out there that do all of that and more.

This book is about you and your marriage. It's about the way your money and your relationship combine to create a Money Relationship. That's right—you and your spouse have a Money Relationship, just like you have an emotional relationship, a spiritual relationship, and a physical relationship.

Every couple recognizes those times when they are emotionally out of sync—one of you is upset and the other person can't understand why. Many of us know how it feels to be at a different place than our spouses when it comes to faith. And what couple hasn't had those nights when one of you is in the mood for some lovin' and the other just wants to fall asleep?

Your Money Relationship is no different. When you and your spouse are making financial decisions—the big ones and the little ones—there will be times when you totally get each other, when you make a plan to spend or save or invest and you head down that financial road together. But if you're like nearly every couple we've ever met, there are other times when your love and your money turn into a toxic mess. You can't agree on a plan or you can't stick to the plans you've made or you just can't understand why your spouse doesn't see things the way you do. Like every other aspect of your relationship, the money piece can either help you grow closer or pull you apart.

We believe that when couples have the right tools and are committed to using them, they can make their love and their money work together to create a thriving Money Relationship and an intimate, solid marriage.

Why Your Money Relationship Matters

We have more than thirty-eight years of financial planning experience between us. We've worked with thousands of couples to help them put together budgets and retirement plans. For a long time, we thought all a couple needed for a solid financial future was a clear budget and healthy savings account. But we were so very, very wrong.

We started to see couples we'd worked with, couples we'd helped create beautiful budget plans that should have sent them into a glorious, happy future, come back into our office on the verge of divorce. All of the perfect plans we'd built with them weren't enough to inoculate them against miscommunication, resentment, and issues like hidden credit cards and secret spending.

Clearly, something else was going on with these couples, something even the best plans couldn't fix. We just couldn't figure out what it was. Then we read a statistic that scared us. We all know that there's a 50 percent divorce rate in the United States, a rate that is not all that different among Christian couples. But here's what we didn't know. Of those divorced couples, nearly 70 percent of them say their breakup was due in large part to money problems.

That number lit a fire in us. If money was at the root of so many broken marriages, and if we knew a thing or two about money, then it seemed that we had a responsibility to use our expertise to help put a dent in this staggering divorce rate. That's why we've spent the last eight years figuring out what it takes for couples to stop fighting about money and start working together to build the life they always dreamed of. And we think we've cracked the code.

It boils down to this: you and your spouse have a Money

Relationship. It's at the core of the way you make decisions about money. Understanding how that Money Relationship works is essential to a thriving, healthy marriage. And that's what this book is about.

The Marital Mix

Recognizing that every couple has a Money Relationship that ripples through their entire marriage was a huge step in our efforts to help couples. The more we dug into this idea, the more we knew it was something far more complex than we first thought.

At the center of every Money Relationship are two people—two different, unique individuals with different, unique ideas and feelings about money. If you and your spouse felt the same way about sex, you'd never argue about sex. If you felt the same way about how to discipline your kids or how often to visit your parents or how important it is to talk through your feelings, you'd never have any conflict. But you don't feel the same way about these things. That's because you aren't the same person. And thank God for that!

But when it comes to a Money Relationship, couples seem to assume they ought to see things exactly the same way all the time, and when they don't . . . well, they wonder why their spouse is such an idiot about money. But here's the thing: every person has a unique way of thinking about and dealing with money—we call this a Money Personality. As we've worked with couples, we've discovered there are five Money Personalities. When two people start building a life together, it's only a matter of time before their Money Personalities start to play into the decisions they make— everything from where to eat dinner to what kind of shoes to buy to what kind of wedding to have.

Discovering your Money Personalities—something you're going to do in chapter 3—will be a revelation in your marriage. It will uncover a part of you that you likely never really thought about before. You'll start to understand that you think about and deal with money in a very particular way, a way that might be nothing like the particular way your spouse thinks about and deals with money. It's going to be one of those aha moments.

You'll have another of those moments when you and your spouse talk about the ways in which your Money Personalities complement each other and clash with each other—that's chapter 4. That ongoing "conversation" about how much you spend on shoes? Now you can get to the root of your different ideas about how much is too much. Your spouse's reluctance to buy you something for Valentine's Day? You might find out there's more to it than your spouse being a jerk.

Sometimes the combination of different Money Per- sonalities can create serious tension and conflict. But when couples know and respect each other's Money Personalities, the results can be beautiful. If you're willing to stick with us, we're going to help you uncover that beauty in your marriage. God created each one of us with very distinct personalities. That beautiful uniqueness is part of our DNA and affects everything we do. It's crucial that we understand that this also includes our approach to money. We believe that this God-given uniqueness is something to be celebrated but also something to be acknowledged, nurtured, and developed *in tandem* with our spouses.

Make It Happen

We have a saying that you'll find throughout this book: "Make It Happen." We believe most couples want a relationship that works. They just need help to break out of old patterns and ways of dealing with money issues. Make It Happen is our way of telling you we believe you have what it takes to change the course of your Money Relationship. We've got the tools to help you, but the motivation will come from you. And we know that if you're serious about making a change, if you are willing to commit to taking an honest look at yourself and your Money Relationship, you can make your Money Relationship something to be proud of. We've seen countless couples recover from years of conflict, secrecy, even separation, and rebuild a marriage that's worth celebrating. If they can do it, you can too.

To make the most out of the tools in this book, we suggest you read it together. You'll be finding out how you deal with money as a person—that's your Money Personality. You'll be discovering potential areas of money conflict in your marriage—we call it the Opposite Dynamic. And you'll be gaining invaluable insight on how to turn those conflicts into cooperation—we'll teach you to Fight Fair. All of this will be far more effective if both of you are reading along and making these discoveries together.

We also suggest taking it slowly. There is a lot of information in the book and we want you to really get each idea before you move on. So don't rush this. The intention is that this book will take you twelve weeks (or ninety days) to get through, so we recommend reading a chapter or two a week and letting the ideas settle a bit before you move on. Talk to each other about what you're reading. See what your spouse is thinking as these ideas start to take hold. At the end of each chapter, you'll find a simple exercise to help you integrate the concepts into your marriage. They're quick and easy, but they're essential to putting all the pieces of the book together. They are a way to Make It Happen.

We also want you to do something else. Before you read another word, we want to make sure you're in this for real. We want you to make a promise to each other that you are ready to change the way you think about and deal with money as a couple. This is a *lifestyle* change, not a short-term plan or a one-shot deal. Like a diet plan or exercise plan, these ideas aren't going to stick unless you decide you are done with the habits that got you to this point. You'll be working on a new way of relating to each other so that you can protect and preserve your relationship.

We're going to be asking you to take an honest look at yourselves and to make some significant changes for the sake of your relationship. When it feels like too much, when you're ready to give up, come back to this promise and remind yourselves that there's nowhere to go but forward. Remember, it takes only ninety days to change your marriage for the better.

If you're committed to doing whatever it takes to discover your Money Personalities and build a healthy Money Relationship, sign here:

By signing my name, I promise my spouse I will work on our Money Relationship. I will be honest, I will be committed, and I will do my best to understand my spouse and respect the differences in our Money Personalities. Together, we can make a change.

_____   _____

Make It Happen!

The Money Couple
Scott and Bethany Palmer

PART 1

• • •

It's All About the Money Personalities

1

When Love and Money Collide

I t all starts with the vows: for richer or poorer. We stand up at our weddings and recite those vows fully expecting that we will happily stand by each other, no matter what. We have big dreams about the life we're starting with this person we love so much.

Every marriage starts with big hopes and dreams. You walk down that aisle celebrating all the beautiful ways you connect as a couple, all those little moments of excitement and joy and intimacy and fun and love and goodness that have been the building blocks of your relationship. And for a while, those hopes and dreams and joys are enough to carry you through the adjustments of marriage.

And then life happens. It doesn't matter if things go along just as you planned or if your plans get derailed early on. The bottom line is that life, no matter how great it is, pushes a lot of our hopes and dreams to the side. You have jobs. You have kids. You buy a house. You lose a house. Your parents get older. You find yourselves stressed out by the present and worried about the future. And over time, through no fault of your own, those dreams you had for your life together get put on the back burner and, one by one, they start to dry up and disappear.

The dream to buy a house? Can't afford it. The dream of going back to school? Not with a baby on the way. The dream of backpacking through Europe? Can't get time off. The dream of retiring at the beach? Not after the market tanked. Whether your dreams are big or small, they tend to fade as the years go by.

Ellen and Jack are a perfect example. When they got married, Ellen was working her way toward a partnership at a small law firm. Jack was a graphic designer and had dreams of starting his own design business. Right away, they started saving so Jack would have some start-up capital when the time came to set out on his own. They had a five-year plan and a common goal. But after they'd been married for two years, Ellen was diagnosed with a chronic illness. Her doctor recommended she cut back her hours at work and try to reduce the stressors in her life. While they had good health insurance through Ellen's job, they still had new expenses to deal with that put a dent in their savings. And that meant Jack's dream would have to wait a bit longer.

As Ellen's illness became more manageable, the job market became less stable. It no longer seemed like a good idea for Jack to venture out on his own, especially when he knew plenty of designers who would do anything for a regular job like the one he wanted to leave. So they waited a little longer.

You can see how this will play out, right? Pretty soon five years have passed. And then they have kids, and then ten years have gone by and the kids need braces or they want to buy a bigger house or Jack's mom dies and his dad moves in with them. After a while, the dreams of those early days just die off.

Now Jack and Ellen would be the first to tell you that they have a great life, that they've made choices they feel good about, and that they are blessed beyond measure. But they also admit that they miss dreaming about the future together. Ellen says, "When we got married, I remember talking about how fantastic it would be for Jack to have his own company and really make his mark in the design world. His eyes would light up when we talked about it. Now most of our conversations are like business meetings—who's doing what and when. I know he wouldn't trade our life now for anything, but I'd sure like to see that look in his eyes again."

There's something life-giving about dreaming together as a couple. It's a reminder that you are stronger together than you are apart. It's a way of saying to your spouse, "I look forward to the future with you."

If you've lost track of the dreams you used to have, we believe you can get them back. We believe you can reclaim the life you envisioned, one dream at a time.

The Money Part

There's a reason we take vows to stick together for richer or poorer. Money ripples into every part of our lives as couples. That's why, whether you have it or you don't, money can test a relationship. If you think about the dreams you had when you got married, most of them have some kind of money component—buying a house, having children, getting a job, moving to a new city, traveling, spending time with friends. Money doesn't equal happiness, but money does play a part in whether our dreams turn into reality. And when money gets between us and our dreams, we get very unhappy and look for someone to blame. And guess who's sitting right there? Yep, our spouses.

We meet with all kinds of couples. And there's a look we see that shows up in couples who have lost their dreams for what their marriage could be. It doesn't matter if they're rich or poor. It doesn't matter if they've been married for forty years or four months. It doesn't matter if they argue constantly about money or if they never talk about money. They sit in our office and barely talk to each other, barely look at each other. When they do speak, their words are filled with blame and resentment and anger. And it's all because life hasn't turned out the way they'd hoped it would.

They come to us because they believe that having a better budget will help. They hope that if they invest some money in just the right ways, they can have that retirement house they dreamed of. But their budget isn't really the issue. We can hand them a budget that's airtight, but if they don't know how to communicate with each other, if they don't know how to work together as they live within that budget, then it doesn't matter how nice their plans are. Their relationship will sink.

Most couples have no idea how to talk to each other about the money component of a decision. They don't know how to compromise or listen to each other or make plans that meet both of their needs. Instead, they fight. They blame each other. They resent each other and hurt each other and hide money from each other. And then they divorce each other.

Reviving Your Dreams

It doesn't have to be that way. Here's the thing: every decision you make as a couple involves money. Every. Single.

One. Money factors into everything from the kind of house you live in to where you go on vacation, from the kind of shampoo you use to the kind of bread you eat. It doesn't matter if we're talking about a $5 cup of coffee or a $50,000 car—money is part of every piece of our lives.

That's why couples who disagree about money will disagree about *everything*.

That combination of love and money is what makes up your Money Relationship. Just like your physical relationship is about much more than sex, and your emotional relationship is about far more than your feelings, your Money Relationship involves a whole lot more than your money. It's about how and why you connect—or don't—when you make decisions where money is involved. It's the deeper set of assumptions and beliefs you bring to your money decisions.

We created this book to help couples stop fighting about money and repair their Money Relationship, regardless of their financial situation. We want to change the way you communicate about money. We want to give you practical, efficient, easy-to-remember, easy-to-apply tools to help you build a stronger Money Relationship. But more than anything else, we want to rekindle your passion for the future—and for each other.

When you started dating, you couldn't help but dream together. You were so excited to learn about each other, to discover your sweetheart's favorite food or most embarrassing moment. You wanted nothing more than to know and understand each other. You could talk for hours, dreaming of the life you'd build together. This is the day to start dreaming again. We believe that every couple can recover the love, intimacy, and dreams they had when they first fell in love.

MAKE IT HAPPEN

Recapture that desire to discover new things about your spouse. Take turns telling each other one thing the other person might not know about you, even after years of being together.

2

Your Money Relationship

We're going to start by really digging into this idea of a Money Relationship. It's kind of ironic that most of the couples we work with have no idea they have a Money Relationship, even though they have come to us to talk about their money and how it's affecting their relationship. It just doesn't occur to people that the way they deal with money as individuals will play into the way they deal with money as a couple.

Instead, couples tend to think that if they just get a really great financial plan in place, they'll stop arguing about money. They think that if they can stick with a budget or get enough put away for retirement or start building their savings that their money problems will be over. But they're wrong. They can fix the budget, stock up for retirement, even load up the savings account and still have a lousy Money Relationship. And what good is the budget if you can't stand each other? What good is that retirement fund or that savings account if your relationship is a mess?

What It's Not

Your Money Relationship has nothing to do with your budget. It has nothing to do with your savings. It has nothing to do with how much debt you have or how much you spend every month. That's your financial arrangement—your debt, retirement, taxes, insurance, investing, estate planning, and so on.

Your Money Relationship is about the daily decisions you make as a couple in which money is involved. (We even put it in italics to show you how important it is!)

Before we move on, we want you to really understand the difference between your finances and your Money Relationship. Your financial plans, your debt, your investments, your taxes, your budget—that's one aspect of your life together. And that's not what this book is about. We want to focus on the relationship *behind* that part of your life, your Money Relationship. That's the part of your marriage that involves all of those little day-to-day decisions about money.

Here's what we mean: Jonell and Kai have been married for fourteen years. They make a fairly good living; he's an accountant at a hospital and she does fund-raising for a small nonprofit organization. They have owned their modest house for eight years. They have a bit of student loan debt left to pay off and one car payment. They tend to use credit cards to pay for nearly everything, but they pay off their cards almost every month. Kai has a 401(k) through work, but they haven't thought all that much about their retirement funds. Their main financial goal right now is to put aside a decent amount of money to help their two children pay for college.

We've given you a pretty good picture of Kai and Jonell's financial situation. You know they have some debt, some savings goals, some money in a retirement fund. You have the basics on their financial life. But those details tell you nothing about their Money Relationship.

When it comes to their Money Relationship, Kai and Jonell have some real challenges. Kai, the accountant, is obviously good at balancing a budget and figuring out where to save and where to spend. So he handles all of the finances in their marriage. Jonell, despite being in a finance-oriented field herself, isn't all that interested in how much they bring in each month or how much they pay out each month. She knows Kai has it taken care of and she doesn't think twice about it.

But Kai worries about their money constantly. Every evening, he looks over their online credit card account to see how much they spent that day. He lies awake, silently calculating where they can cut back to make sure they pay off the bill that month. Those rare months when they have to settle for a minimum or partial payment feel like a failure to him.

If Jonell buys a new outfit for a fund-raising event, Kai mentally cancels his plans to take her out for a nice dinner later that week and quietly resents Jonell for pushing their monthly budget to its limits. He worries that they won't have enough for their retirement, much less enough to help the kids with college. He's considered talking to Jonell about his concerns, but he knows she gets defensive when they talk about money. So he keeps his worry to himself.

While their financial picture is perfectly healthy, their Money Relationship is anything but. He's a wreck, she's clueless, and neither of them has any idea that this is a crisis in the making. It won't be long before Kai either explodes at Jonell for her spending or develops an ulcer from worrying about it. And Jonell doesn't get a free pass here. Her willingness to wash her hands of the family finances isn't a sign of trust; it's a sign of disrespect for Kai. Why should he bear the full weight of decisions that have an impact on the whole family?

Most couples have no idea that there's a difference between their finances and their Money Relationship. So when they try to solve financial problems that are really the result of a troubled Money Relationship, they end up

frustrated. Unless couples get to the root of the problem—
the challenges in their Money Relationship—they just can't
move forward.

We worked with a couple who had been married for
more than forty years and had been clients with our financial
planning company for most of those years. One afternoon,
they came in for an appointment and announced they were
getting a divorce.

All their financial plans were in place and had been for
a long time. But behind those perfect plans were resentment
and hurt feelings and misunderstanding. The problem was
that they never understood that they thought about money
in very different ways. So every decision they made in those
forty-plus years just added another straw of resentment to
the proverbial camel's back. Their plans were solid but their
relationship had fallen apart.

They had plenty of money and they'd managed it fairly
well. The problem? She thought they needed more money
in their retirement accounts and he didn't. She'd been
anxious about their future for years and had nagged him
about putting more away. But he thought they'd be fine
and had stopped listening to her concerns a long time ago.
The closer they got to retirement, the more anxious she
became until she couldn't take it anymore and she bailed.

On the surface, their impending divorce was the result
of poor financial planning. But it wasn't their assets that

were the problem. It was their total lack of communication. We've never seen a couple break up over their 401(k) performance. We've never seen a couple get divorced because they didn't have enough life insurance or because their estate planning wasn't complete or because they didn't pay off their student loans in less than five years. What kills relationships is miscommunication and misunderstanding. That's especially true when it comes to money because, as we've said, it has an impact on every aspect of life.

We often ask couples to tell us about the last money decision they made. Most of them come up with some investment or a savings plan or a big purchase. But when we ask them to think smaller, they start to see that they are dealing with money almost from the moment they wake up.

Think about it. Do you take a long shower or a money-saving short shower? Coffee at home or a fancy coffee from the place on your way to work? Generic cereal or the name-brand stuff? Drive to work or take public transportation? Bag lunch or out to eat? Squeeze in some overtime or go back home to the family?

If you and your spouse have fundamental disagreements about money—how much to spend, how much to save, how much risk is too much—then each of those little, seemingly innocent decisions about hot water and coffee and lunch are fraught with meaning. Take a long shower when your spouse is trying to cut back on the utilities and you've just created a problem. Grab breakfast at the fast-food joint when you've agreed to an eat-at-home budget and you've stirred the hornet's nest.

Because money trickles down to just about every decision we make during the day, it's not surprising that couples clash over money. It's like a constant pop quiz, one you're bound to fail unless you and your spouse have a strong Money Relationship.

Breaking the Cycle

What we see over and over again is couples who are caught up in a cycle of assumptions, misunderstanding, and blame. It doesn't matter if they have a healthy bank account or are deep in debt. Because money isn't the problem. Their Money Relationship is the problem.

It took us years to see this, not only in our marriage, but in our work. We'd been in the financial planning business for a decade before we realized that something wasn't working. We'd meet with couples, put together airtight financial plans for them, and still see them fighting, stressing out, and even divorcing because of their financial issues. And we didn't get it. We thought that once we gave them a plan, their conflict would go away. But it didn't.

That's when we realized there was something else going on. It wasn't the money itself that created these issues. It was that couples had no idea how to talk about money in a way that helped them work together to build the future they'd always dreamed of. We'd been focusing on the "how" behind their money plans instead of the "why."

What we didn't realize is that it's not enough to have your financial ducks in a row. You need to know why you think about and deal with money the way you do. And that's what this book is all about.

Think about the last time you and your spouse argued about money. For most couples, those arguments are rarely about the money itself. Instead, they are about deeper relationship issues like trust and respect and connection.

Take Mitch and Karen, for example. Mitch loves his coffee. Loves it. If he can't start his morning with a twenty-ounce double shot from his favorite coffee shop, his whole day is off. But Karen doesn't understand why Mitch would pay almost six bucks a day to feed his habit when she brews a great pot of coffee at home every morning for pennies. She's tired of watching Mitch spend more than $100 a month on something she sees as totally unnecessary. One morning she lets him know he needs to cut back.

Here's how that conversation goes:

KAREN: You've got to stop hitting the coffee shop every morning. It's too expensive.
MITCH: It is not. Besides, I love their coffee.

KAREN: I make coffee here every morning. Why can't you just drink that?

MITCH: It's not the same. What's the big deal?

KAREN: The big deal is that it costs too much!

MITCH: It's a few bucks and it makes me happy. What's wrong with that?

KAREN: This isn't about your happiness. It's about you spending too much money.

MITCH: Why are you so cheap all the time? I just want to get a cup of coffee!

KAREN: I'm not cheap! I'm trying to keep us from spending money we don't have!

MITCH: This is ridiculous.

So he walks away feeling controlled; she walks away feeling disrespected. They're both hurt and upset. And not because of the money.

Disagreements like this go to the heart of your relationship. They are the kind of conflicts that linger—every time Mitch heads to the coffee shop, he's going to be irritated at Karen all over again and she's going to get mad at Mitch all over again. This is the kind of conflict that gets worse over time because couples simply don't know how to fix it. And since every decision you make as a couple has a money component, conflicts like this come up over and over and over again. It's a terrible cycle.

But you can break that cycle by learning to understand your Money Relationship.

Bringing Love and Money Together

Your Money Relationship isn't about the plans you make with your money. It's about the reasons you make those plans. You save for a house because you dream of settling down together. You save for college because you dream of a bright future for your children. You plan for retirement because you dream of traveling together one day. You buy lavish gifts for your spouse because you dream of showing her how much she means to you. You clip coupons and buy day-old bread because you dream of keeping your family financially secure.

You and your spouse started your lives together with those dreams. So now it's time to do what it takes to reclaim those dreams, to quit arguing about money, and to heal your Money Relationship.

We aren't therapists, but we have worked with thousands of couples as they've tried to repair their Money Relationships. Over and over, we've seen that when a couple's Money Relationship isn't working, nothing else in the relationship is working either. But when couples know how to communicate about money, when they understand each other's approach to money, when they build a strong Money Relationship, the rest of their relationship grows stronger too.

We want to show you how your love and money come together and help you create a lifestyle that works. We know it's not always easy to turn a relationship around; it takes time to change old habits and replace them with patience and grace and understanding. And it takes intentional effort to break out of the cycle of blame and frustration and learn to really listen and rediscover each other. But we believe you can do this. We've seen so many couples come back from the brink of divorce by making the decision to repair their Money Relationship. Whether you've been married five months or fifty years, we are confident you can be one of those success stories too.

Our hope for you as you work your way through this book isn't that you come away with more money in your bank account. It's that you come away with a strong, healthy Money Relationship.

MAKE IT HAPPEN

What are three decisions you made this week? What was the money component? Remember, it's not just the big decisions that involve money, but the little ones too.

3

Getting to Know Me: The Five Money Personalities

No one is neutral about fruitcake. You either love the stuff or you hate it. No in between; no grey area. On Team Fruitcake, you are all in or all out. You don't even have to think about it to know which side you're on. You just know.

Money works the same way. There are people who hate to spend money. They feel real, physical pain when they spend more money than they think they should. And there are people who love to spend money. They get an adrenaline rush just thinking about their next purchase. There are people who have no qualms about risking everything they have on a big investment and people who would rather stuff all their money in their sock drawer than take a chance on a six-month CD or a low-risk investment. Then there are those people who never think about money. They spend it when they have to and save it if someone reminds them to, but they have no emotional ties to their money. It's a non-issue in their lives. You don't even have to think about it; you know just which one you are.

We both love to spend money. It doesn't matter if we have money or not—even in our leanest years, we couldn't wait for the chance to spend money. It doesn't matter how much we spend—getting a couple of doughnuts for a buck feels as good as buying a car (okay, almost as good). It doesn't matter whom we spend it on—we're as happy buying gifts for friends or donating to a good cause as we are buying something for ourselves. But we know people who hate to spend money, people who cringe at dropping a couple of dollars in the office birthday pool, people who would rather eat a stale sandwich for lunch than grab a burger at the drive-through. And for a long time, we didn't get it. Why were these people so cheap? Didn't they know how to enjoy life? Didn't they want to be generous?

Then we figured something out: people have very different ways of thinking about and dealing with money. Now that might seem sort of obvious, but here's the thing: most of us assume that everyone thinks about money like we do, and those who don't, well, they're wrong.

Bethany's mom is a great example. She is the queen of saving money. If she has a choice between a brand name and a generic item, she'll always go generic. She's the woman who buys day-old bread at the bakery. And here's the thing—she doesn't do it begrudgingly. She loves it! She can afford to buy name brands and fresh bread. It's not a matter of how much money she has. It's that she truly enjoys saving money. If she can pay less than the other guy, she's thrilled. The woman loves a deal. And not just the deals she finds for herself. She gets just as excited when someone else finds a bargain. When Bethany scores a pair of killer shoes on clearance, her mom is as happy as if she'd gotten them herself. There is just something in her that loves to save money, whether she saves ten cents on generic cereal or 80 percent on a designer dress.

Other people are like our friend Carla. She doesn't think about money, doesn't care about money, doesn't worry about money. She doesn't think to balance her checkbook until her bank statement shows up in her e-mail in-box. She's a freelance writer and sometimes forgets to invoice her clients. She couldn't tell you how much she has in her savings account or even if she has a savings account. Forget planning for retirement or college for her kids. Not on her radar. She's always happy to get something on sale and she's not reckless with her finances. She just doesn't give her money much thought.

Both Bethany's mom and Carla deal with money in ways that are vastly different from the way we deal with it. But that doesn't mean our way is superior—as much as we're tempted to think it is. Bethany's mom doesn't understand how we can just decide to go out to eat without a long conversation about how much we're going to spend. From her perspective, our ideas about money are as odd as her ideas seem to us.

We all know people with vastly different spending habits than our own. Everyone has that "cheap" friend who never seems to pay for anything, or the coworker who throws in a five on a group gift when everyone else is throwing in a twenty, or the coupon queen who never met a deal she didn't like. We all know people who seem to spend indiscriminately—the "shopaholic" who can't resist one more purchase, the big-spending buddy who always buys another round.

We know people who will always take a financial bet—investing in the latest multilevel marketing business or buying shares of some company they know nothing about in Sri Lanka. We know people who've planned for every possible problem the future might hold—flood insurance and fire insurance and dismemberment insurance and pet insurance and on and on. And we know people like Carla, who don't think about money at all.

The bottom line is that everyone thinks about and deals with money in a unique, highly personal way. That's because each of us has something we call a *Money Personality*. There are five of them:

Saver   **Spender**

Risk Taker   **Security Seeker**   **Flyer**

Each of the five Money Personalities has its strengths and its challenges. Each of them can help you make great financial decisions, and each of them has the potential to get you into financial trouble. That's why we remind people that there is no right or wrong Money Personality. They are what they are. So the goal in discovering your Money Personality isn't to point out your flaws. It's to help you understand yourself and the way you think about and deal with money. Because the more you know about yourself and your perspective on money, the better equipped you are to work with your spouse to build a strong Money Relationship.

Finding Your Money Personality

Before we dig in any deeper on the Money Personalities, we want you to read through the descriptions below and figure out which of them seem to fit you the best. You're actually going to choose two of the five—a Primary Money Personality and a Secondary Money Personality. As you read through the descriptions, you'll find one that strikes you as absolutely true to who you are when it comes to money. That's your Primary Money Personality. There will be a second one that hits close to home as well, but isn't quite as strong. That's your Secondary Money Personality.

For example, Scott's Primary Money Personality is Spender. He can spend money with the best of them. His Secondary Money Personality is Security Seeker. When there's an investment to be made, Scott will always think about throwing in some money—that's his Spender side—

but because he's also a Security Seeker, he'll do a ton of research on the investment before he commits. Even then, he's likely to say no if the risk is outside his comfort zone. His primary approach to money is to spend, but he's also careful about *how* he spends.

For a long time, we thought people had just one Money Personality. But the more we looked at ourselves and our Money Personalities, the more we realized that these Money Personalities aren't mutually exclusive. You can be a Saver and a Risk Taker, a Spender and a Flyer, a Security Seeker and a Saver. Not only is it possible to have more than one; it's highly likely! We'll talk more about how your Primary and Secondary Money Personalities work together in the next chapter. For now, all we want you to do is identify your Primary and Secondary Money Personalities. We'll get to the nitty-gritty soon enough.

Your Primary Money Personality—the one that really drives your thinking about money—will be easy to figure out. You'll instantly recognize yourself in the descriptions below. Your Secondary Money Personality is less obvious, but it often shows up when you're feeling stressed about money. So if you're a Saver who worries you won't have enough money in the bank to cover you in an emergency, you're probably a Saver/Security Seeker. If you're a Saver who skimps on the little things so you can afford a splurge now and then, you're probably a Saver/Risk Taker.

If you aren't sure or you just want more details about each type, you can find a free Money Personality Profile on our website, TheMoneyCouple.com. With the help of statistical scientist Dr. Kirk Cameron, we've developed this tool to confirm your Money Personalities. This simple quiz will take you less than fifteen minutes to complete, but the results will have a profound impact on you and your relationship.

Name:

Primary

Secondary

Once you've figured out your Primary and Secondary Money Personalities, have your spouse do the same. You'll both need this information as you work through the remaining chapters of the book.

The Money Personalities

Saver

 Ed is a Saver. How do we know? Well, Ed is the kind of guy who washes his Ziploc bags. He reuses aluminum foil. If he finds a piece of rotting fence in an alley, he brings it home and tucks it away in his workroom in case he finds a use for it later. He has little plastic bins full of old faucets and knobs, jars of rusty screws and bent nails, three hammers that he got at a garage sale for a dime apiece, and at least three old lawn mowers he is pretty sure he can fix.

If Ed sounds a lot like your grandpa, well, he is. Except that Ed is a thirty-eight-year-old high school physics teacher.

Like most Savers, Ed never met a deal he didn't like, but for Ed, free beats cheap every time, even if the thing he's getting is old, broken, or useless. He'd rather recycle that old rotten fence into some sort of woodworking project than buy new stuff at the lumberyard at half price.

Ed's junk collection is just the tip of his Saver iceberg. He drives a car with no heat, his driver's side door doesn't close all the way in the winter, and it's missing its ignition panel. He has to start it with a screwdriver. Most of his wardrobe is made up of clothes he's had since college and shirts his wife buys him for Christmas. His favorite shoes are a pair of high-end loafers he got at the thrift store for $7—a bit more than he likes to spend, but his wife convinced him they were a very good deal.

Ed is, obviously, a fairly extreme example of a Saver. Not every Saver is a pack rat. Not every Saver objects to buying something new. We know Savers who wear nothing but designer labels—that they bought at a deep discount. We know Savers who are worth millions, and they got that way by watching every penny. We know Savers who drive nice cars and live in nice houses and go on nice vacations—all of them paid for up front, in cash.

While Savers don't always save in the same ways, there are some traits that are common to most Savers. You're a Saver if you:

GET A GENUINE RUSH FROM SAVING MONEY. It's a source of pride to get something you wanted for less.

ARE ORGANIZED, RESPONSIBLE, AND TRUSTWORTHY WHEN IT COMES TO FINANCES. A Saver won't tap out the kids' college fund to pay for a new boat. A Saver won't toss a $20 into the office basketball pool.

RARELY SPEND IMPULSIVELY. Savers will scour the Internet for deals, plan every detail of a vacation, and make sure they have the money in hand before making a purchase.

AVOID CREDIT CARD DEBT LIKE HEAD LICE. Savers hate paying interest and accruing debt. They want to pay off every bill, in full, right away.

As we mentioned, every Money Personality has its

challenges. If you're a Saver, you need to be aware that you can be:

A JOY STEALER. If you're a Saver and your partner isn't, your resistance to spending money can suck the fun out of everything from seeing a movie to going on vacation.

OVERLY FOCUSED ON FINANCIAL GOALS. Often, the reason Savers are joy stealers is that they tend to think about only the money. It's great to have firm financial goals and to work hard to meet them, but sometimes Savers need to swallow their anxiety and let themselves—and others— just enjoy life.

CHEAP. A Saver has a hard time parting with her money, so much so that she comes across as cheap and even selfish to others.

Savers can be great partners because they are careful about spending and usually spend wisely. The challenge is for them to see money as a means to an end, not an end in itself.

Spender

 Colleen is a Spender. If there's a chance to spend money, she'll spend it. Friends coming over for dinner? That's the perfect excuse for a bundle of fresh flowers and some cute new dessert plates. A Saturday running errands? Might as well invite a friend to lunch at the café to break up the day. By May she's already got a closet full of Christmas gifts. And you know those displays right by the checkout counter at every store? Colleen can't resist them—she'll grab a pack of gum, a little toy for her daughter, a couple of packs of lip balm, whatever looks interesting or new or necessary.

For Colleen, spending isn't about having more stuff. She's far more likely to buy a gift for a friend than to spend money on herself. She is the first to pick up the tab when she has coffee with a friend, always shows up at a party with a lovely gift for the host and hostess, and has a reputation for giving generously when there's a need in her church community or her children's school.

Colleen's spending has gotten her into some financial pickles. She has bounced a few checks in her time, and she amassed a fair bit of debt before she was married and handed the finances over to her husband. But she's learned that she doesn't have to spend a lot of money to get that rush of joy that comes from shopping and giving. Those little items from the checkout line make her just as happy as the cart full of big-ticket items.

Spenders don't care how *much* they spend or who they spend it on. They aren't necessarily rich; we know Spenders who can do some serious shopping at the dollar store. Spenders just like spending. You're a Spender if you:

LIVE IN THE MOMENT. Spenders are focused on what's happening right now, and they are willing to spend money to make life a blast. They might have less money down the road, but for the Spender it's all about making great memories today.

LOVE TO BUY THINGS FOR OTHER PEOPLE. Spenders get a lot of joy out of giving gifts, helping out, and treating other people.

GET A THRILL FROM THE PURCHASE. It doesn't matter if you're shopping at Saks or at the Salvation Army thrift store. The price doesn't matter. It's the fun of buying that counts.

If you're a Spender, you need to be aware that you can be:

IMPRACTICAL. Spenders are often impulse buyers. A Spender walks into a store without lists, without limits. Spenders don't do research to find a good deal; we don't wait for a sale. If we want something, we get it—and Spenders don't differentiate between wants and needs.

NONCOMMUNICATIVE. All that impractical impulse buying means that Spenders don't think—much less talk—through purchases with their partners. This lack of communication can come across as secretive and sneaky to the Spender's spouse.

FILLED WITH REGRET. We're both Spenders, so Christmas is a blast! But January 15 is never pretty. We don't regret the purchases or the fun we had buying them and giving them, but we regret getting carried away.

A BUDGET BREAKER. A Spender can put together a mean budget. And he can have great intentions of sticking to it. But Spenders rarely do. That can lead them—and their unwilling spouses—into serious, life-altering debt. Spenders might even feel bad about overspending, but they have a hard time stopping themselves. This can be unbearably frustrating to the Spender's spouse.

A Spender can be a great partner because she will never let finances get in the way of truly living life to its fullest. The challenge for the Spender is to respect the money expectations of her spouse, particularly if that person is a Saver.

Risk Taker

 You've probably met someone like Patrice. She's that person who is always up to something interesting. When she goes on vacation, it's never somewhere like Florida or the Grand Canyon. No, Patrice heads to a beach in Vietnam or goes ice climbing in Canada. When she goes out to eat, it's to that new place that opened in a warehouse downtown or a little hole-in-the-wall joint you've never heard of. She's the first to try out a new tech gadget, the first to tell you about some band she discovered at a music festival in Tucson, the first to bike to work in the snow.

Patrice is a Risk Taker, not just in her travel plans and restaurant choices, but in her finances as well. She's not afraid to invest in a friend's business venture or chip in to help a buddy make his independent film. She has a good job and a healthy disposable income, and she sees no reason to let her money sit in a bank account when she can use it to be part of something amazing or intriguing or innovative.

She has taken a hit more than once. She and a friend of a friend went in on a food cart business that never really took off, and now she's the proud owner of an industrial-grade chest freezer. She bought a house in desperate need of rehab with the intention of flipping it, but the housing market tanked and she's stuck with a house she can't sell. Despite these financial setbacks, Patrice is always looking for the next big thing, the next opportunity to plunge head-first into an adventure. One of these days, she knows it's going to play out perfectly.

For Risk Takers, the thrill of jumping into a financial challenge doesn't just come from a huge payout on an investment; it comes from taking the risk in the first place. Even if they never hit it big, Risk Takers never give up on following that rush they get from trying out a new idea, even if it costs them everything. It's just how they're wired. If you're a Risk Taker you:

ARE A BIG-PICTURE PERSON. Risk Takers aren't always worried about details. They don't get hung up on the *how* of an idea. Instead, they get a bead on something—a business opportunity, an investment option, a real estate deal—and they move. Fast.

LOVE FINDING THE NEXT ADVENTURE. For Risk

Takers, no idea is too out there, no risk too big. Their sense of adventure takes over and they want in.

GET EXCITED BY POSSIBILITY. Risk Takers get more excited about the idea of something than about the thing itself. By the time the deal plays out and they've got their return, they've moved on to the next big idea.

LISTEN TO YOUR GUT. More than conventional wisdom or financial experts, intuition is what a Risk Taker trusts. If a deal doesn't feel right, she won't do it. But if something strikes her, she's on it.

AREN'T AFRAID TO MAKE DECISIONS. Risk Takers don't mess around when it comes to money. They make a decision and make it fast. That can be a real plus when there are important decisions on the line.

If you're a Risk Taker, you need to be aware that you can be:

BLINDED BY POSSIBILITY. When a Risk Taker gets a hold of an idea, reason has left the building. And with it go concern for other people's feelings, attention to details, and long-range planning.

EASILY RESENTED. Even if a Risk Taker is in a relationship with another Risk Taker, the quick decisions and the leveraging of assets can end with two people who don't like each other very much. When a decision pays off, everyone's happy, but all it takes is one bum deal to create a rift of resentment.

IMPATIENT. The Risk Taker can lose patience with people who don't sign on to her big ideas as quickly as she'd like. Risk Takers make decisions without consulting the people those decisions affect most—their spouses.

INSENSITIVE. Risk Takers hate feeling hemmed in by other people, so rather than work for compromise, they charge ahead and deal with the relational fallout later. And when the Risk Taker's spouse isn't on board with the decision, there is always relational fallout.

A Risk Taker can be a great spouse because she is always thinking about the future. The challenge for the Risk Taker is to keep her spouse involved in the risk-taking decisions and to be willing to say no to a deal.

Security Seeker

 If ever there was a classic Security Seeker, it's Jerry. He eats breakfast at the same restaurant every Saturday. On Casual Fridays at work, he wears one of his three blue V-neck sweaters and khaki pants. His favorite vacation spot is Orlando, Florida, where he owns a small condo.

But all that predictability doesn't mean Jerry is boring. Not at all. He's always up for an adventure, as long as he can plan for it. When a group of college buddies decided to ring in their fortieth birthdays together by renting a sailboat and spending five days on the ocean, Jerry was right there with them. When his anniversary rolls around every year, his wife knows he'll come up with something over-the-top romantic—a surprise weekend getaway, a couple's spa day, or a piece of custom jewelry she's been hinting about.

Like so many Security Seekers, Jerry has no problem spending money; he just wants to make sure he's spending wisely. That vacation property? He didn't bite until the price was right and he knew his family would want to spend time in the Dells for years to come. The sailing trip? Jerry mapped out their course, researched rental companies to find one with a solid reputation, and made sure his life insurance was up-to-date. The gifts for his wife? He makes sure their yearly budget includes room for this annual splurge by cutting back on extras for a few weeks. So while he's willing to spend money, he's not willing to jeopardize his family's future to do it.

Security Seekers like to know the future is settled and safe. They are all about planning, consistency, and clear expectations. When it comes to money, the Security Seeker's motto is "The safer, the better." He loves a sense of order and predictability. You're a Security Seeker if you are:

AN INVESTIGATOR. A Security Seeker would never invest in a piece of property he hasn't seen. In fact, a Security Seeker wouldn't just need to see the property; he'd need to have the soil tested for toxicity, look into all the zoning restrictions within a three-mile area, and get a detailed pro-spectus from the developer and a resumé from every other investor.

TRUSTWORTHY. Security Seekers rarely put their futures on the line. That means they aren't likely to spend this month's mortgage on a car or tap into the college fund to join a multilevel marketing company.

WILLING TO SACRIFICE. A Security Seeker would rather do without today than do without tomorrow. Security Seekers won't spend money until they know they've got enough to pay the bills, contribute to their retirement, and cover any other obligations they've set up to make sure the future is taken care of.

PREPARED FOR ANYTHING. Security Seekers are never caught without a plan. The Security Seeker rarely ends up in a crisis (at least not a real crisis—that 5 percent stock market dip can feel like a crisis to the Security Seeker), which means the rest of the family can rest a little easier.

If you're a Security Seeker you need to be aware that you can:

BE OVERLY NEGATIVE. Security Seekers get nervous about risk, so they often say no to every idea that comes along. The Security Seeker can become controlling, using his veto power to keep his spouse from exploring her own dreams.

GET STUCK IN A RESEARCH RUT. We call this tendency "paralysis by analysis." In other words, Security

Seekers can get so caught up in avoiding buyer's remorse or making sure an opportunity is foolproof that they never act.

STIFLE CREATIVITY. This challenge doesn't just affect other people in the Security Seeker's life; it affects the Security Seeker too. Over time, that need for security can become so all-consuming that she stops looking at the possibilities and sticks with the certainties—and that can be a very subtle form of control.

The Security Seeker can be a great spouse because his careful planning and steady approach to money can help couples avoid disaster. The challenge for the Security Seeker is to resist making decisions out of fear and to know how much financial security is enough.

Flyer

 Finally, we get to the mysterious Flyer. Take Brett, for example. He's a musician—he plays in a couple of bands, teaches music, and works in a recording studio as a sound engineer and producer. He lives a fairly unconventional life, and he wouldn't have it any other way.

Brett has lived in at least ten different apartments in five different cities since graduating from college fifteen years ago. He tends to go where the work is and makes a life for himself when he gets there. For the last three years, he and his wife have lived in a great old house, but he's starting to get antsy. One of his coworkers told Brett about a studio his friend owns in another state, and Brett and his wife are seriously considering making a move.

Brett's students would be sorry to see him go. He's a gracious, passionate teacher, and he is truly invested in the success of the kids he works with. Their parents love him too. He is easygoing, encourages the kids to work hard and practice, and isn't picky about when they pay him or even how much they pay him for lessons. One of the parents has offered to help Brett set up a more reliable billing system, but Brett thinks that's more work than it's worth. He always gets paid eventually and he really doesn't have a head for business, so he'd just as soon avoid the headache of billing and keeping accounts.

The Flyer is perhaps the most unusual Money Personality. Flyers don't think about the money component of a decision—at all. They're not anxious about it; they're not consumed by it; they have absolutely no emotional response to money. You're a Flyer if you are:

BASICALLY CONTENT WITH YOUR LIFE. A Flyer might be dirt-poor and living in an Airstream out by the highway, but he doesn't care. As long as a Flyer is making his own choices, he's happy.

BIG ON RELATIONSHIPS. For Flyers, relationships and connections with other people are crucial.

HAPPY TO LET SOMEONE ELSE TAKE CARE OF YOUR FINANCES. This can be a big plus in relationships, especially if the other partner has one of the other Money Personalities.

NOT MOTIVATED BY MONEY. Most Flyers end up living exactly the lives they want to live because they make choices based on what they want, not what will make them the most money.

If you're a Flyer you need to be aware that you can be:

REACTIONARY. Flyers don't think about money, but money is a necessary part of life. So sooner or later, even Flyers have to pay attention to their bills or their looming retirement. And when they do, they often make decisions based on fear, not good advice.

LACKING IN THE SKILLS NEEDED TO SOLVE YOUR MONEY PROBLEMS. When money problems come up, the Flyer tries to handle it herself. But because she doesn't care about money, she doesn't have any idea how finances work. Interest? Consolidation? Refinancing? Comparison shopping? These concepts aren't on her radar.

DISORGANIZED. Flyers aren't always disorganized people in the general sense, but when it comes to money, they are all over the place. We've asked Flyers to bring in tax returns and they have no idea where something like that might be. Some of them don't even remember if they filed taxes or what their taxable income is.

UN-RESPONSIBLE. Anyone who isn't a Flyer might think Flyers are irresponsible. But really, they are *un*-responsible.

Irresponsibility suggests a deliberate lack of maturity. But Flyers aren't trying to be lazy or inattentive. They genuinely don't think about money issues.

Flyers can make great spouses because they are fairly easygoing about money issues. They aren't going to be controlling or uptight about finances. The challenge for Flyers is to stay involved and invested in the family financial picture.

So where did you find yourself in these descriptions? As you go through the rest of this book, we'll keep coming back to your Money Personality, so make sure you have a sense of who you are.

And don't forget to identify both a Primary Money Personality and a Secondary Money Personality. The interplay of these two has a big impact on your Money Relationship, so it's important that you know what they are and have a fairly good sense of how they play out in your life.

(Be sure to take the full Money Personality Profile at TheMoneyCouple.com!)

One more note: Now that you have identified your Primary and Secondary Money Personalities, you've probably already figured out which of them fit your spouse too. But stop right there. It's essential that you let your spouse determine his or her Money Personalities. Part of the process of healing your Money Relationship is for both of you to know yourselves well and understand why you think about money the way you do. If you just assign your spouse a Money Personality without really letting him or her work through the options and own that Money Personality, the rest of the ideas in this book won't be as effective.

It's easy to read these descriptions and think about all the issues that can come up when couples have different Money Personalities, and we'll get to that soon. But for now, we want to keep the focus on you as individuals and make sure you truly understand your own Money Personality and how it affects you.

Your Lens for Life

Your Money Personality is the lens through which you make money decisions. It's what motivates you to wait until that sweater is on sale. It's what drives you to put 30 percent of your paycheck in your savings account. It's what makes you buy a round of drinks for your buddies. And since money touches every decision you make, your Money Personality frames your perspective on life.

We find that people who are Spenders tend to be fairly gregarious. They live large. They are generous not only with their money but with their time and their talents as well. Spenders love to lavish affection and attention on the people they care about. They are the kind of people who insist you stay with them when you're visiting instead of going to a hotel. They are the ones who offer to drive when you go on double dates or let you choose the restaurant and still insist on paying. They are just bighearted people. They aren't necessarily outgoing, but they are always ready to help out and do what they can for the good of other people.

Savers tend to be more intentional about their money and the other parts of their lives. They rarely make a decision without a lot of forethought. They like plans and clear expectations about relationships, work, even their free time. Savers have a good sense of how much time or effort a project will take and will dole out their energy accordingly. That's why Savers often cultivate a tight circle of friends— in their own way, they conserve their relational "funds" as deftly as they conserve their money.

The Security Seeker and Risk Taker Money Personalities create unique lenses for life as well. Security Seekers are, obviously, unlikely to take risks—personally or professionally. They like to know what's coming. When they plan a vacation, they want to see all the maps, read all the brochures, make all the reservations. Risk Takers are happy to get online and see if there are cheap tickets for the next day to anywhere in the world; they can be packed by morning! A Security Seeker loves to settle in for a cozy movie night at home while a Risk Taker will head to the movie theater and pick a flick on site.

And Flyers? Well, Flyers are content to go with the flow. They have ideas and opinions, to be sure, but they tend to be easygoing and spontaneous. At work, they are often highly creative and easily adaptable. They don't stress out over deadlines and they aren't easily frazzled. In relationships, they let their true feelings show but don't get too worked up over disagreements or conflict. They like to keep things simple and clear.

Naturally, these are broad generalizations, but you get the idea. Of course, there are spontaneous Savers and selfish Spenders, confident Security Seekers and nervous Risk Takers. But it's important to recognize that your Money Personality isn't a separate piece of you; it's fully integrated into other parts of your personality, and vice versa. The deeper your recognition of the ways your Money Personality influences your life and your decisions, the more prepared you are to dig into your Money Relationship and make it stronger.

Take Britt and Alex, for example. They love to travel. But almost every time they go on vacation, they end up in a huge argument that ruins the whole trip. They hate it, their kids hate it, and until last year, they had no idea how to fix it. But once Britt and Alex figured out their Money

Personalities, they started to break the cycle of conflict that was killing their relationship.

It turns out that Britt is a Saver and Alex is a Risk Taker. They realized that many of their vacation arguments started when Alex went shopping for souvenirs. They loved bringing home reminders of their travels, but they had very different ideas about what those reminders should be. Alex loves to collect art and pottery made by local artists. Britt is happy with a refrigerator magnet and a postcard.

But after they discovered their Money Personalities, Britt and Alex had a better sense of why they both felt so strongly about a seemingly trivial issue. For Alex, buying a painting or a ceramic jar from a local artisan was a thrill— who knows what that artist might accomplish one day? He loved the idea of investing in an unknown artist and being part of that person's success. For Britt, her concerns about the money Alex spent far outweighed any appeal the purchase had. She saved and planned their vacation budgets very carefully and had every meal and excursion accounted for. In one afternoon of shopping, Alex could ruin months of her hard work.

So instead of arguing at the gift shop, Britt decided to talk to Alex about her anxiety. She suggested they set a limit on the cost of any souvenirs. Alex agreed. So Britt factored that money into their travel budget, and they had their first fight-free vacation in years.

That's what happens when you know your Money Personality. You can figure out why you become frustrated or angry or controlling or anxious and then do something about it. You suddenly know why it drives you crazy when your spouse goes into the store for a gallon of milk and comes out with milk . . . and doughnuts and a magazine and some batteries and three bags of chips. And you suddenly know why you feel controlled when your spouse gets mad at you for buying doughnuts and a magazine and some batteries and three bags of chips.

Your Money Personality DNA

When we talk with people about their Money Personalities, they always ask us where their Money Personalities come from. Are you born with them? Are they a response to how you were raised? The answer is yes.

We've come to believe that your Money Personality is part of your DNA. Now there's no Money Personality gene, but the way you think about money seems to be something you're just born with. When we look at our two sons, it's obvious to us that Cole is a Saver and Cade is a Spender. Cade can't keep a dollar in his pocket to save his life. If he finds a dime on the ground, he starts thinking about what he can buy with it. And since we're Spenders ourselves, we totally get it.

But Cole is our Saver. The poor kid lives with three people who know how to spend some serious coin, but he is just naturally inclined to save his money. When our Saver son was younger, he started talking about wanting to buy a cool car some day. Scott told him that when the time came, Scott would match Cole's savings dollar for dollar. That was before Scott knew just what kind of kid he was dealing with. A few years later, our eleven-year-old has almost two thousand dollars in the bank. At this rate, we're going to have to sell *our* cars, and maybe our house, to keep Scott's promise.

The family you grew up in can have a big influence on how you feel about money, but we find that most people can look back and see signs of their Money Personalities in their childhoods well before they would be intentionally responding to their parents' influence. As we've said, Bethany's mom is a serious Saver, but Bethany can see that she was always a Spender. Even as a little girl who was unaware of her mom's spending habits, Bethany was always ready to spend her allowance on whatever was in front of her.

Your Money Personality is as much a part of you as your feelings about fruitcake, and they're just as unlikely to change. So don't fight it. Embrace your Money Personality and start paying attention to all the ways it plays out in your life. The more you know about how you view money, the better equipped you are to overcome your challenges and start using your strengths to build a better Money Relationship.

MAKE IT HAPPEN

Think about a time when your Primary Money Personality has driven a money decision. Do the same for your Secondary Money Personality. How have those Money Personalities been an asset in your life?

4

The Opposite Dynamic

Your Money Personality frames the way you think about money—and about life. Once you know your Primary and Secondary Money Personalities, you'll start noticing them playing out in all kinds of ways. If you're a Risk Taker, for example, you'll start to notice the little decisions you make every day that have an element of the unknown to them—checking out a new restaurant, pursuing a new business contact, trying a new recipe. If you're a Saver, you'll notice that you compare prices at the grocery store or automatically head to the clearance rack when you're shopping.

But that's just your Primary Money Personality at work. Your Secondary Money Personality, while not as prominent as your Primary Money Personality, still has an impact on the way you view money. That's why there are Spenders who experience serious buyer's remorse and Flyers who retire as millionaires.

We've learned that there are certain combinations of Primary and Secondary Money Personalities that create something we call the *Opposite Dynamic*. The Opposite Dynamic is the internal conflict so many of us experience when our Primary and Secondary Money Personalities clash.

Our friend Matt's Primary Money Personality is Spender. His Secondary Money Personality is Security Seeker. His Spender side loves to shop. So a few months ago, when Matt needed a new speaker for his home theater system, he spent his Saturday morning at the electronics store, did a little looking to find just what he wanted, and left with a new speaker. And a new flat-screen TV. And a new Blu-ray player. And a Wii.

For the first five minutes of his drive home, Matt was on the new-stuff high that Spenders feed off of. And then his Security Seeker side kicked in. What had he just done? What was he thinking, spending so much? What if he needed that money next week? What if the car needed repairs? What if he lost his job? By the time he got home, he'd already figured out what he could return and vowed to never let himself spend so much again.

Matt's response is the result of the Opposite Dynamic. His Primary and Secondary Money Personalities lead him to want two very different things—the thrill of the purchase and the security of knowing he has planned for the future.

The Opposite Dynamic is the result of your Money Personalities having competing needs. That competition creates internal tension. And that tension can quickly creep into your Money Relationship. So we're going to take some time to break down this idea of the Opposite Dynamic so you can see how that internal tension might be seeping into your marriage.

Clashing Personalities

The five Money Personalities can be put into two groups. On one side are the Spender, the Risk Taker, and the Flyer. These three Money Personalities have a few things in common:

- They think of money as a means to an end.
- They tend to be more impulsive.
- They don't experience much fear or anxiety when it comes to money.

On the other side are the Saver and the Security Seeker. They also have a few things in common:

- They think of money as an end in itself.
- They tend to be intentional spenders.

- They struggle with fear and anxiety when it comes to money.

Saver   Spender

Security Seeker   Risk Taker

Flyer

If your Primary Money Personality is in one group and your Secondary Money Personality is in the other, you have the Opposite Dynamic. And while there are plenty of benefits to the Opposite Dynamic, most of us are more likely to notice the challenges it creates.

Our friend Claire's Primary Money Personality is the Saver and her Secondary Money Personality is the Flyer. She got a new job recently, one that called for a more professional wardrobe. That meant Claire needed to go shopping. And Claire hates shopping. So she put it off until the weekend before her first day at the new job. Instead of having time to look for a good deal or wait for a sale, Claire ended up paying full price for clothes she didn't really like all that much. And instead of feeling confident in her new outfit on that first day of work, all Claire could think about was how much it cost.

Claire's Saver Money Personality created anxiety about how much she'd spent on the clothes, but it's her Flyer Money Personality that kept her from making plans that could have helped her spend less in the first place. That's the Opposite Dynamic at work.

Like Matt in the earlier example, Claire is dealing with that internal tension between her Primary and Secondary Money Personalities. And while it's often easier for people to pay attention to the conflict they feel because of the Opposite Dynamic, we find that the Opposite Dynamic can also be a helpful diagnostic check. If you pay attention to it, it can save you from the challenging parts of your Money Personality.

Every one of the five Money Personalities has a downside. Spenders can go off the deep end and leave themselves and their families drowning in debt. Savers can be so aggressive in their efforts to save money that they can rob themselves and everyone around them of the joy that comes from living life to the fullest. Risk Takers can be reckless and Security Seekers can be so fixated on the future that they never enjoy the present. Flyers can find themselves working for thirty years and having nothing to show for it—no house, no savings—nothing.

Your Secondary Money Personality works as a kind of stopgap that keeps your Primary Money Personality from running amok, and vice versa. Take Matt, our Spender/ Security Seeker. Matt's Secondary Money Personality keeps him focused on the future. When he spends more than he planned to on new electronic gear, his Security Seeker side kicks in and helps him get back on track so that when the car breaks down—because it will—he'll be ready for it.

At the same time, Matt's Spender Money Personality helps Matt keep an eye on the here and now. Matt's not so worried about tomorrow that he forgets to enjoy today, even when that means spending some money to make that enjoyment happen. His Opposite Dynamic works to his advantage.

If we look at Claire, we can see that her Opposite Dynamic can be an asset as well. She's a Saver, something that can be a lifesaver for a Flyer. Flyers aren't necessarily careless with money, but they don't think about it much. So if a Flyer is also a Spender, he can end up in all kinds of financial trouble—unpaid bills, deep debt, foreclosure. For Claire, her Saver Money Personality helps keep her from spending money she doesn't have.

At the same time, Claire's Flyer Money Personality keeps her Saver side from falling into a spiral of shame and anxiety when she does spend more than she planned. Claire worried about her new-job shopping spree for a morning and then she moved on—other things are far more important to Claire than her money.

If you have the Opposite Dynamic between your Primary and Secondary Money Personalities, it might take a little thinking to see how your conflicting ways of thinking can actually help create balance in your life. But once you start to see how the two work together, you'll be moving toward a better understanding of the role you play in building a strong Money Relationship with your spouse.

In the next two chapters, we're going to move from talking about each of you as individuals to dealing with the way your Money Personalities combine as a couple. That's why it's so important to know yourself well before moving on. We want you to know and own both the good and the not-so-good aspects of your Money Personality, as well as understand how the Opposite Dynamic plays out in the decisions you make about money.

MAKE IT HAPPEN

Think of three examples of times your Primary and Secondary Money Personalities have worked together in a positive way. If you have the Opposite Dynamic, think about ways your Primary and Secondary Money Personalities balance each other out.

5

The Big Reveal: The Five Money Personalities Together

Every couple we know argues about money—including us. Money has an impact on every decision you make, so it only makes sense that some of those decisions will lead to fights about money. For a lot of couples, those fights get personal—"You spend too much!" "You're cheap!" "You're too controlling about the money!" "I don't trust you with our money!" It's no wonder money conflicts are behind more than 70 percent of the divorces in this country.

There's also something deeply personal about money fights. When we first started helping couples with their Money Relationships, we knew everyone had a Money Personality. We knew couples argued about money. But we didn't realize how hurtful those arguments could be. In the last ten years of working with couples, we've come to see that there is something about a person's Money Personality that runs into the core of who that person is. Your Money Personality is part of the lens through which you view life. So when someone criticizes that view, it feels deeply personal.

That's why we're going to spend the next couple of chapters helping you and your spouse discover each other's Money Personalities. We believe that when you truly understand each other and your perspectives on money, you can stop blaming each other, stop criticizing each other, and start working together to build a healthy Money Relationship.

(**Take a free Money Personality Profile at TheMoneyCouple.com.**)

Before we move on, we want to make sure you and your spouse have identified your Primary and Secondary Money Personalities. Obviously, it's best if both of you are reading this book, but if you're reading it on your own, you can still get your spouse involved.

Here's what not to do: *do not* guess your spouse's Money Personality. Yes, it might be obvious that your honey, who buys a new pair of shoes every time he goes to the mall, is a Spender, but let him figure that out for himself. And *do not* tell your spouse you already know exactly what Money Personality she's got. She might keep her money stuffed in a grocery bag at the back of her closet, but don't tell her she's a Security Seeker. Let her discover it on her own. Nothing feels worse than having someone else decide who you are.

The only way to build a solid Money Relationship is for both of you to know and own your Money Personalities, and that can't happen unless you both take the time to understand your perspectives. So instead of ending up in a thirty-minute fight, send your spouse to our website (TheMoneyCouple .com) to take a ten-minute quiz and discover his or her Money Personality. Then you're ready to keep reading!

A Crowded Marriage

Once you and your spouse have identified your Primary and Secondary Money Personalities, take a minute to write them out and make a little chart. We'll use ourselves as an example to show you what we mean:

	Scott	Bethany
Primary	spender	spender
Secondary	security seeker	risk taker

Now take a minute and really look at your chart.

	Name:	Spouse's Name:
Primary		
Secondary		

Can you see it? It's your Money Relationship in a nutshell. Seeing your Money Personalities laid out like this is a revelation, a major wow moment. For the first time, you can see why those little disagreements about money seem to turn into major arguments. Look at all those Money Personalities at work!

This chart is a kind of map for your Money Relationship. It shows you what you're dealing with. We've known about our Money Personalities for a long time, but the first time we wrote them out like this, it was a huge moment of discovery. We'd never really thought about the fact that there are *three* different Money Personalities at work in our relationship, and that at any given time, those three are bumping into each other in ways we had never understood before.

Sometimes we're the Spender and the Risk Taker. Sometimes we're the Spender and the Security Seeker. And sometimes we're the Security Seeker and the Risk Taker. Now that you know a bit about the five Money Personalities, you can probably guess where we run into potential conflict. We can go shopping for Christmas gifts for our boys and have a blast—our Spender sides get along great! But on the ride home, Scott's Security Seeker comes rising up and starts to freak out about the money we've dropped.

If it sounds as though we have multiple personalities in our house, we do. And so do you. We've spoken with thousands of couples and we have yet to meet one where both spouses have the same Primary and Secondary Money Personalities. When it comes to money, opposites really do attract.

Naturally, that can create tension in a relationship. And we'll look at that more closely in the next chapter. But for now, we want you to just sit with this idea of multiple Money Personalities. Think about the implications for your relationship. Sure, there is potential for conflict. But there is also tremendous potential for maximizing the strengths of your various Money Personalities, not just in terms of your finances but in your relationship in general.

Learning the Language

Knowing your Money Personality gives you huge insight into why you think the way you do about money. Knowing your spouse's Money Personality gives you huge insight into your spouse. And isn't that what makes relationships hum? Knowing each other and really getting what makes the other person tick?

That's why there's more to your Money Relationship than your financial plans. Every time you make a decision, you're bringing your perspective on life to the table. And nothing feels better than making decisions with someone who understands and respects your perspective.

If you've ever traveled someplace where the locals don't speak the same language as you do, you know how frustrating it can be to try to bridge the language barrier. But when you finally find someone who speaks your language, it's such a relief! You feel heard and understood.

The same thing happens when you and your spouse understand each other's Money Personalities. It's as though you've learned how to speak the same language. And speaking your spouse's language is a great way to demonstrate your love and respect. Scott knows I'm always willing to take risks with our money. I know those risky decisions make him nervous. But when I tell him about a potential investment and he says, "Let's go for it!" he is speaking my language. And it means the world to me.

It took us a long time to get to the point where we understood each other well enough to really listen when the other person expressed fear or anxiety or frustration about a financial decision. But getting to know each other this way has added a whole new level of trust and closeness to our relationship. The same can happen for you.

Walk a Mile

If you're struggling to understand your spouse's Money Personality, we want to suggest a simple—and maybe even fun—exercise. Take a day and try to live out your spouse's Money Personality. No being snarky here—"Hey, look at me, spending all the money we don't have because I'm a Spender!" No, this has to be an honest attempt to learn something new about this person you married.

So some weekend soon, choose your days—one of you gets Saturday, one of you gets Sunday. Then go about your day, but have the assigned person talk out loud about the money decisions he or she is making. Let's look at a couple where one of them is a Spender and one is a Saver. On Saturday, they're both going to live like the Spender. Here's how that day might look:

They wake up and get dressed for the day. The Spender looks in his closet and says, "Okay, so when I look at my clothes, I see a bunch of stuff I'm tired of wearing. I like to feel good about how I look, so my first thought when I get dressed is that I could really use some new shirts. And then I think about when I could go shopping to get them."

The Saver's heart is starting to race at the idea that her spouse is *already* thinking about spending money and they haven't even left the bedroom! But because this couple is committed to understanding each other and healing their Money Relationship, she sits on the edge of the bed and listens. She might even say—as kindly as possible—"Wow, honey, I had no idea you started thinking about spending money so early in the day."

The Spender is then likely to suggest going out for brunch because, well, why not? And again, the Saver's blood pressure will rise. But love is going to take over and she's going to go with it. As this couple moves through their day, the Spender is going to keep talking about what he's thinking and why he's thinking it. And the Saver is going to listen and do everything she can to learn about her beloved's perspective.

On Sunday it's the Saver's turn. So when this couple wakes up, the Saver might say, "It's kind of cold in here, but I like that because it reminds me that we're doing a good job keeping our heating bills lower than last year. And that feels good to me." Now it's the Spender's turn to keep his lips zipped and discover the inner workings of his spouse's Money Personality.

As they go through the morning, this couple makes more decisions that involve money: Will they grab coffee on the way to church? How much should they put in the collection plate? The youth group is having a bake sale to raise money for their mission trip. Will this couple buy some brownies or not? And the Saver is going to talk her honey through her thought process on every one of these choices. By lunchtime, the Spender husband is going to be amazed at how heavily money decisions weigh on his Saver wife.

We want to be clear: we're not telling you to go out and spend money you don't have or to give your spouse free rein to destroy your finances in a day. If you'd rather make hypothetical decisions, that's fine. You could say something like, "If we went into your favorite store right now, what would you do first?" The point of this exercise is to build understanding and even a bit of respect for your spouse's Money Personality, and you can do that without spending a cent.

For so many couples, their Money Relationship is a tangle of false assumptions, old resentments, and constant blame. At the root of all of that is a misunderstanding of who the other person is and why she behaves the way she does. But when these couples discover their Money Personalities and take the time to really understand each other, they begin to see past those assumptions and resentments. And that's when they can see what's really happening in their Money Relationship.

Seeing What's Real

That chart you filled out earlier in this chapter? We call it the "Big Reveal" because it uncovers the underlying dynamics at work in your Money Relationship. It's easy to use this information to start placing blame and criticizing your spouse. When we speak to large groups of couples and have them do the Big Reveal, we see most of them exchange a look that says, *Now we know who's causing the problems. It's you!*

But we want you to flip that idea on its head. Instead of using this information as a weapon to blame your spouse, use it as a tool to rebuild a better Money Relationship. Use it to deal with the *realities* in your relationship instead of the assumptions and labels and fears in your relationship. When you do, you can repair years of pain and relational damage.

Fred and Heidi came to one of our seminars with a long history of money conflict. They told us this seminar was their last-ditch effort to solve their money problems and avoid getting a divorce. Yes, that was a little bit of pressure! We took them through the Money Personality Profile and found out that they had four of the five Money Personalities in their relationship. Heidi was a Saver/Risk Taker and Fred was a Spender/Flyer.

It turned out that Heidi controlled their finances because she was afraid Fred would spend all their money, money she needed to keep her small business afloat. So she had Fred on an allowance.

But Fred, on the other hand, had a bank account Heidi didn't know about, one left over from his bachelor days. He didn't really intend to use it once they got married, but he never got around to closing it. When Heidi started talking about how much money she needed for her business, Fred started putting money in that account just to have a little backup in case Heidi's plans fell apart.

There was a lot of anger and mistrust in this relationship. Fred told Heidi she was a control freak. Heidi was livid about the secret account. We got them calm enough to take the Money Personality Profile, and while it didn't solve all their problems, it did serve as a revelation. It turned out that Fred had deep-seated fears that Heidi would use up all their money, and Heidi acknowledged that they weren't simply paranoia—her business was risky and it was a good idea to keep some of their money out of it. Fred admitted that he was wrong not to trust Heidi with their money; she was a savvy businesswoman and had made them a lot of money with her risky investments. It was the insight they needed to turn their relationship around.

If you want to fix your Money Relationship, you have to know what's real. You have to break out of the cycle of blame and start seeing the situation from your spouse's point of view (see the appendix for The 5 Money Personalities Survival Guide), and the only way to do that is to know each other's Money Personalities. When you do, you can start to see why your spouse makes the decisions he makes. You can see the ways her Money Personality has helped your family. You can appreciate the time and effort and thought that goes into your spouse's money decisions. And you can start to extend grace to your spouse.

When that happens, you might find that you've begun to heal far more than your Money Relationship. In some ways, all of this work is like going back to those early days of dating, the days when there was no one as fascinating to you as your sweetheart. You wanted to know everything about each other—her favorite flower, his favorite kind of socks, the story behind that scar. No detail was too mundane, no story too silly. It was important and interesting because it was part of this person you loved.

Once people get married, we tend to stop discovering each other. We get to that place of familiarity and forget that our spouses are deep wells of quirks and dreams and ideas that are still worth discovering. So let the work you're doing on your Money Personalities feed your interest in your spouse. Let it reinvigorate your curiosity about this unique and special person you married. Even if he's been driving you nuts with his spending, even if she's making you crazy with her coupons, try to look at the person behind those behaviors and find that sweetheart who, not so long ago, was everything to you.

At the beginning of this book, we talked about how important it is for couples to dream together. We know how quickly daily life can steal those dreams you had when you first got together—dreams about this person you love, dreams about the future you'd build together, dreams about work and family and travel and the mark you'd make on the world. But you can get those dreams back. Understanding your Money Personalities is like a deposit in the dream bank. It's a solid step forward on the road to a better Money Relationship and a better marriage.

MAKE IT HAPPEN

Over the next week, try to make three decisions about money as though you had your spouse's Money Personality (either the Primary or Secondary one). Over dinner, talk about what you learned during this experiment.

6

Opposites Attract

Karen and Jamal started dating when they were in their late twenties. Jamal had a great job with a law firm and Karen was in grad school. Karen loved Jamal's sense of adventure, his free spirit, and his generous heart. He would treat total strangers to coffee on his morning java run. He spent almost every weekend hiking or exploring a new place. And he loved to surprise Karen with gifts—a scarf he knew she'd had her eye on, flowers in the middle of winter, and eventually, a stunning diamond engagement ring.

Jamal loved Karen's sense of purpose, her drive to make the world a better place. She worked hard and focused intensely on everything she did. He loved her commitment to her friends, her family, and her work. He loved that she had big ideas about her future, and he wanted to be part of those plans. She was like a steady ship in his sometimes-chaotic life.

Everything was great. And then they got married.

It wasn't long before Jamal and Karen found themselves with very different ideas about how to handle their money. Jamal wanted to take Karen on a postgraduation trip to India. He thought it would be a great way to celebrate her accomplishments. Karen knew it would be only a few months before she had to start paying her student loans, and she wanted them to start saving money now so they could pay those loans off in three years.

They were only a few months into their marriage when they hit a wall of misunderstanding and blame. Karen thought Jamal was living in dreamland and he needed to start being more responsible with their money. Jamal thought Karen was a stick-in-the-mud who worried too much about money.

Linda and Ted had been married for nearly thirty-five years when their Money Relationship exploded. For most of their marriage, Ted had worked and Linda had stayed home with their three kids. Linda wasn't interested in their finances; they had everything they needed and more, and that was all she needed to know.

Ted and Linda had been high school sweethearts. They got married when they were both twenty and essentially grew up together. They had highly defined roles in their relationship, and they both liked it that way. From the day she met him, Linda loved Ted's strength and the way he took care of her and, eventually, their children. He was kind, decisive, and smart, but he also had just enough of a wild side to make every day with him an adventure. He taught her how to ski, how to fish, how to build a fire, how to shoot a basket. He made her feel protected, cared for, and loved.

Ted was attracted to Linda from the get-go. She was sweet, funny, and thoughtful. When they were teenagers, she'd bake him cookies, cheer for him at basketball games, and listen patiently when he was disappointed in a grade or a game. He could be a little wild sometimes, but Linda helped him feel grown-up and smart. She seemed to see the best in him, and that felt great.

While Ted was in college, Linda worked three different jobs to help keep them afloat. Once he graduated, he promised her she'd never have to work another day in her life, and he'd made sure to keep that promise by taking a secure job with an insurance agency, one where he knew he could make a good living and take care of his growing family.

But one afternoon, long after the children were grown and gone, Ted came home in the middle of the day and told Linda he had some bad news. It turned out that Ted was about to be fired. The problem, he told her, is that he hadn't been honest with her about their finances. He had tapped into their retirement account years earlier to help pay off their mounting debt. He'd hoped to work another ten years to make up the difference, but now he didn't know what to do. He didn't know if he would be able to find another job, certainly not one that paid what he'd been making. And they didn't have the savings they needed to weather a season of unemployment.

Needless to say, Linda was stunned. As they talked, Ted came clean about his mistakes with their money, mistakes that had left them in danger of losing their house and nearly everything Linda thought was safe and secure.

After her initial shock wore off, Linda was, understandably, livid. How could he keep this from her? Why didn't he include her in these decisions? Why did he wait until it was too late to come to her? Ted confessed that he'd never told her about any of this because he didn't want to worry her. He knew she'd trusted him to take care of her and instead he'd destroyed their lives.

We hear stories like this all the time. Two people meet and fall in love. In those early days, their differences are what bring them together. But once they have a few years and a whole lot of money decisions under their belts, those qualities that were so attractive when they were dating have become a source of conflict in marriage. Sometimes it's an obvious clash, as it was for Jamal and Karen. And sometimes it's lurking just beneath the surface, only to erupt like it did for Linda and Ted.

We have found that roughly 90 percent of the couples we work with have an Opposite Dynamic in their relationship. That doesn't surprise us a bit. There's something subconscious in the way we are drawn to the opposite Money Personality. We recognize that this other person will add something important to our lives. A Security Seeker might be drawn to the Risk Taker because the Risk Taker brings the thrill of the unknown into the Security Seeker's predictable life. A Spender might be drawn to a Saver's sense of responsibility and stability. A Saver might be drawn to a Flyer's generosity. Whatever it is, it seems that when it comes to Money Personalities, the old adage is right: opposites attract.

Bring Back the Attraction

A strong marriage is only possible when couples reclaim that attraction, when they stop seeing the downsides of their differences and start loving the way they complement each other. But that can't happen until you take an honest look at how your Money Personalities affect your Money Relationship.

Remember the Opposite Dynamic from chapter 4? On one side of the scale we have the Spender, the Risk Taker, and the Flyer. On the other, we have the Saver and the Security Seeker.

Saver

Spender

Security Seeker

Risk Taker

Flyer

Many of us have the Opposite Dynamic in ourselves.
Our Primary Money Personality is on one side of the scale

and our Secondary Money Personality is on the other side. The same thing happens in couples.

The vast majority of the couples we work with have the Opposite Dynamic in their relationship, and it's often that Opposite Dynamic that causes conflict. Take Joe and Ann, for example.

In the Big Reveal, their Money Personalities lay out like this:

	Ann	Joe
Primary	spender	saver
Secondary	security seeker	risk taker

They have four of the five Money Personalities at work in their Money Relationship. That's a lot of potential collisions.

For the most part, Joe and Ann have a strong relationship. But the little differences between them are starting to add up to increased tension in their marriage. That's because every decision they make involves their competing Money Personalities.

- Ann wants to go skiing over the holiday break. Joe is content to stay home and have a staycation.
- Ann wants to try out a new restaurant. Joe wants to stick with the value menu at their neighborhood burger place.
- Joe is thinking about starting a small business. Ann is scared they'll lose their hard-earned savings.

The Opposite Dynamic in Ann and Joe's relationship means they see the world through very different lenses. And the differences are wearing them down as a couple.

Because every couple has as many as four Money Personalities at work, the Opposite Dynamic adds an interesting layer of complexity to your Money Relationship. So we've put together a simple way to figure out just how many Opposite Dynamics you have in your relationship. Once you know the answer, you'll be able to see just where the tension might be coming from in a conflict about money.

Here's how to figure it out:

1. Go back to the results of your Big Reveal in chapter 5.
2. Starting in the top left corner and moving clockwise, count every instance of the Opposite Dynamic.

Start Here

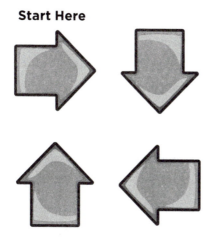

So Ann and Joe's Opposite Dynamics would look like this:

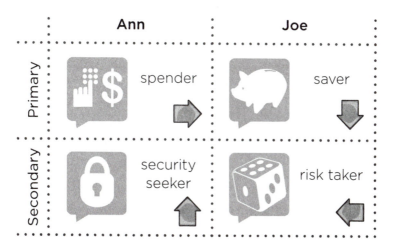

As you can see, Ann and Joe have four Opposite Dynamics in their relationship:

Between Spender and Saver = 1

Between Saver and Risk Taker = 1

Between Risk Taker and Security Seeker = 1

Between Security Seeker and Spender = 1

Total: 4

There's no right or wrong number of Opposite Dynamics. We have two in our relationship and it doesn't make us any more or less prone to conflict than other couples. What matters isn't the number but your awareness of these potential areas of disagreement and misunderstanding. Knowing where you see things a bit differently can go a long way toward helping you make money decisions with care and kindness.

Once Joe and Ann discovered that they have four Opposite Dynamics in their marriage, they could see that their arguments about money weren't really about money at all. Their argument about where to go on vacation wasn't about the merits of skiing versus the joys of staying home. It was about Ann wanting to do something fun and Joe feeling that they couldn't afford to take an expensive vacation right now. Once they got to the heart of the matter, Joe agreed it would be nice to get out of town but suggested a week at a cabin a few hours away where they could cross-country ski for half the price of a trip to the mountains. Ann loved the idea. Joe set a budget, and they did some research and found the perfect place.

Choosing a restaurant stopped turning into a fight and became a chance for them to break some bad habits. Instead of going out to eat because they didn't feel like cooking, they decided to splurge on a couple of great meals a month rather than eating at the most convenient place twice a week. So Ann's Spender Money Personality got to indulge a bit while Joe's Saver could feel good about reducing their eating-out expenses. And with the option of a quick bite at a restaurant off the table, they discovered that they liked making simple meals together at home. As a Risk Taker, Joe loved to try new recipes and Ann was happy to be his guinea pig.

The small business Joe hoped to start had been a real point of contention for these two. It pushed all of Ann's Security Seeker buttons, and for a long time, she was not willing to budge on her refusal to free up money for this risky endeavor. But after talking through their Opposite Dynamics, Ann decided she was willing to keep talking about it. It was still too big a leap for her to just say yes, but she no longer refused to consider the possibility. For Joe and Ann, being able to move this conversation from the "too hot to handle" category of marital decisions to the "let's keep talking it through" category was a huge step in a positive direction.

Seeing the ways the Opposite Dynamic plays out in your marriage isn't a free ticket to no more conflict. It's a way to recognize that those conflicts don't have to get personal or painful. You can address problems as partners, not as adversaries, because you know that the other person is coming at the problem from a legitimate perspective that just happens to be different from yours. And when you know that, you can work through problems with respect and a true desire to find middle ground.

We're often asked if there is a Money Personality combination that just doesn't work. The answer is no. The differences in your Money Personalities are never insurmountable, not if you're both committed to understanding each other and respecting each other and willing to remember what it was about those differences that attracted you in the first place.

It isn't the differences between you and your spouse that create tension in your Money Relationship. It's the nitpicking, the controlling, and the assuming that cause problems. The good news is that you can change that. You can change the way you talk to each other and the way you make decisions. It's all about finding the strengths of your Money Relationship.

Stronger Together

Just as your personal Opposite Dynamic helps you keep your Money Personalities in check, the Opposite Dynamic in your relationship can be a huge advantage. Bethany and

I have the Opposite Dynamic in our Secondary Money Personalities—she's a Risk Taker and I'm a Security Seeker. That's why I have a paper bag next to our bed.

There's something about bedtime that gets Bethany's mind reeling with possibilities. It's not unusual for her to climb into bed and turn to me with this look in her eyes that I know means I'm about to hear a big idea. When she tells me she's heard about an opportunity to invest in a doughnut franchise in Estonia (I wish I were kidding), it's time for me to breathe into that paper bag so I don't hyperventilate from fear.

When these conversations come up, both of us are running on pure emotion. Bethany is all excited because there's a deal in front of her and she's ready to grab hold of it. I'm trying not to freak out and it's all I can do to just keep breathing. But despite all that emotion, we don't fight about this stuff anymore—at least not very often. That's because we understand each other and the way our Money Personalities work.

I know that Bethany is a Risk Taker and that she gets a thrill out of the potential in front of her. That doesn't mean she's already sold our house to buy a doughnut shop in Estonia. It just means she's excited by the possibility. And she knows that I'm a Security Seeker who gets nervous about staking our future on a breakfast pastry. But she also knows my initial reaction won't be my only reaction. So we are able to listen to each other, talk through our options, and respect the other person's needs. Bethany needs to know I'm going to hear her out. I need to know she's not going to do anything without having me on board.

What's more, we've learned that we make far better decisions together than either of us would make on his or her own. If I weren't there to talk through these ideas with Bethany, she'd probably own a doughnut store in every city in Siberia. And if she weren't there to push me out of my comfort zone, I'd have all of our money invested in savings bonds and we'd be living in my parents' basement.

It hasn't been easy for us to get to this point. We've had plenty of painful arguments about money. And we will probably have them again. But they are far less likely to happen now that we understand how the other person thinks about money.

It's so easy to think of your spouse's Money Personality as a giant *No* stamped on your dreams. The Spender feels hemmed in by the Saver. The Saver feels out of control because of the Spender. The Risk Taker feels limited and the Security Seeker feels threatened and the Flyer feels controlled. But if you're willing to shift your perspective and see your partner's Money Personality as an asset in your Money Relationship, you'll find yourselves moving forward with the belief that you are stronger together than you can ever be on your own.

MAKE IT HAPPEN

Think about the ways your Money
Personalities combine with your spouse's,
and answer these questions:

- How many Opposite Dynamics does your
  relationship have?
- What challenges do your opposite
  Money Personalities create in your Money
  Relationship?
- What are some ways you can use Opposite
  Dynamics to make better decisions
  together?

Finally, tell your spouse one thing you appreciate
about his or her Money Personality.

PART 2

...

The Heart of the Matter

7

Your Money or
Your Wife

If all that's at stake in your Money Relationship is your financial picture, we wouldn't be writing this book. There are plenty of resources out there to help you put together a balanced budget or get out of debt or invest well. But we are convinced that your budget, your debt, and your investments are not the real issues in your relationship. What's at stake is not your money; it's your relationship.

If it were just about the money, it wouldn't hurt so much when your spouse says you're cheap. You wouldn't be so angry when your spouse spends more on groceries than you'd budgeted. You wouldn't feel so ignored when your spouse starts a business even though the risk scares you to death.

But it does hurt and we do get angry and we do feel ignored. Because it's not about the money.

We worked with a couple who had a great plan for saving money. They each had a small cookie tin on top of the fridge. The idea was that they'd put a little spending money in their tins each week—a buck or two here and there—and they got to use it however they wanted. So she had her tin and he had his tin.

The husband was a golfer and he had his eye on a high-end driver. He saved his spending money for months to buy this golf club. Finally, he knew he had enough to make the purchase. So that weekend, he pulled his tin down from the fridge, opened it up, and found . . . nothing. It was empty.

He went to his wife and asked her if she knew what had happened to his money. She said, "Oh, I used it." He didn't even have the words to ask her what she'd used it for. It didn't matter what her answer was. It didn't matter that he could save his money again and get his driver in a few months. He told us, "I felt like she'd cheated on me." It wasn't the loss of the money that hurt. It was the loss of trust in his wife that left him devastated. They'd had a deal, and she ignored it—and him. That's what hurt.

This was the story that convinced us that there is something profoundly painful about the ways in which couples hurt each other when it comes to money. It's serious enough that we started calling this kind of behavior *financial infidelity*.

Are You Cheating?

We use the term *financial infidelity* to refer to a host of money-related behavior: lying about money, hiding money, secretly hoarding money, controlling money, or anything that involves one spouse being less than honest with the other.

We have yet to meet a couple who has no financial infidelity in their relationship—we have it, you have it, we all have it. While we hear lots of stories of terrible, blatant financial infidelity, it isn't always intentional. It isn't always a huge, devastating secret. Some financial infidelity is relatively innocent.

And sometimes it doesn't involve much money. Maybe you tell your spouse you spent "about fifty bucks" on a birthday present for your mother when you really spent $75. That might not seem like a big deal, and maybe from a purely financial perspective it isn't, but it's still financial infidelity.

Financial infidelity is far more pervasive and complex than we once thought. We've found that 65 percent of women have a secret credit card or a secret stash of cash. Now before any of you guys start getting suspicious of your wives, you need to hear the next part. The majority of these women said they set up these accounts because they were concerned about their families' finances. They didn't trust their husbands to make good financial decisions for their families.

Still want to ask your wife about it?

Financial infidelity, like sexual infidelity, usually starts out with a small breach of trust. It's like the office affair that starts with conversations around the watercooler, then turns into lunch, then turns into dinner, then turns into a sexual relationship.

Financial infidelity can start out small and snowball. You say you're going to spend $100 and you spend $200. You keep a little secret stash of cash in your underwear drawer, a stash that goes from $50 to $100 to $500 to $5,000, and you never tell your spouse about it.

But some financial infidelity, the kind that does the most damage in a relationship, is meant to be hurtful. It's the secret credit cards, the intentional lies about spending, the total control over the finances, the hidden accounts. That's the stuff that pushes marriages to the brink of divorce—and beyond.

It's Not the Money

The emotional toll of financial infidelity is far more devastating than the toll it takes on your money. You can figure out how to recover from overspending. You can find a way to get some money put away for retirement. You can work through almost any money problem. But it takes a whole other kind of repair work to recover from the loss of trust that comes from financial infidelity.

We know a couple who ended up divorced after the wife discovered her husband had rung up tens of thousands of dollars in debt on a secret credit card. But it wasn't the debt that pushed her to leave him. She didn't care about that. It was the total breakdown in communication, in their partnership, in trust. It's not about the money. It's about the relationship.

Financial infidelity hurts because it goes to the heart of a relationship. It's a breach of trust, a sign of indifference, a lack of respect. And that hurts, no matter how much money is involved.

But we've seen couples heal from the pain of financial infidelity. We've seen them agree to put an end to lies and control and secrets and start over again. We've seen couples who were emotionally bankrupt start reinvesting in their relationship and rebuilding the dreams and plans that brought them together in the first place. It takes patience, grace, and a tremendous commitment to break old habits, but you can make it happen.

There's a little financial infidelity in every relationship, and in the next chapter we're going to help you get to the root causes of financial infidelity in your marriage. But before you can put an end to it, you need to know how it worked its way into your Money Relationship.

We have put together something we call the Financial Relationship Index (FRI), and you can find it at TheMoneyCouple.com. Before you read the next chapter, use the FRI to measure the amount of financial infidelity in your relationship. It's best if you and your spouse each take it separately and talk about your scores *after* you've finished this book. In other words, you aren't going to reveal your scores to each other right now. You're taking the FRI so that each of you can get a clear look at what's going on in your Money Relationship.

It's absolutely essential that you are brutally honest on the FRI. You can't heal what's broken in your Money Relationship unless you face it. So answer the questions honestly. We're going to give you some suggestions on how to talk through your results with your spouse, so don't worry about that part. Instead, take a deep breath and get ready to put an end to the secrets and lies and little deceptions that have the potential to destroy your Money Relationship and your marriage.

And please keep in mind that your score isn't a sign of how close you are to divorce. The fact that you're on chapter 7 of this book means you are serious about changing the direction of your Money Relationship. But your score will give you a good picture of where you are and where to focus your efforts as you work through the remaining chapters.

MAKE IT HAPPEN

Go to TheMoneyCouple.com and fill out the Financial Relationship Index. Does your score surprise you? Are there things you do that you never thought of as infidelity before? What can you do to be more honest in your Money Relationship?

8

The Roots of
Financial Infidelity

The point of uncovering financial infidelity in your Money Relationship isn't to point fingers or place blame. It's to help you and your spouse understand what's really happening in your relationship so that you can get rid of everything that's holding you back from a strong, healthy marriage.

In the same way that understanding your Money Personalities helps you and your spouse stop assuming the worst about each other, understanding how and why financial infidelity creeps into a relationship will allow you to name it and deal with it. That's how you get the trust back. That's how you grow closer as a couple. That's how you reclaim all those dreams you had.

The FRI will give you a score that lets you know how much financial infidelity exists in your relationship. But it won't tell you what that financial infidelity is really all about or how to fix it. That's what we'll cover in the next few chapters.

There are five main reasons couples commit financial infidelity:

1. Financial Separation
2. Overspending and Debt
3. Lack of Planning
4. Control
5. Money Secrets

Whether you have a lot of financial infidelity or a little, whether it's intentional or accidental, it's crucial to understand why it happens and how you can keep it from destroying your marriage.

Financial Separation

Whenever we start talking to a group about financial separation as a cause of financial infidelity, we almost always see a hand shoot up in the audience. "Are you saying it's wrong to have separate checking accounts?" The answer is no.

We don't have a problem with separate checking accounts. There are plenty of good reasons to have them. Maybe you have one for personal use and one for business use. Or one for his expenses, one for hers, and one for both.

You can have twenty-five checking accounts, fifteen credit cards, and four savings accounts for all we care. It is important to be transparent with what is coming in and what is going out of those accounts.

Not long ago, we were in the airport, waiting for a flight. There was a couple who looked to be in their sixties sitting behind us at the gate. They were in the middle of a heated conversation and we couldn't help but overhear them. Evidently, she had some bank account that was separate from him. She had put a significant amount of money into this account, around $100,000. And he was furious.

> HIM: I don't know anything about this bank or these people. Why didn't you just put it in the other account?
>
> HER: I didn't think it should go there. It needed to be in this account.
>
> HIM: But I don't know this bank at all. Who are these people?
>
> HER: It's not a problem. It's going to be fine there.
>
> HIM: You don't know that. I want to talk to someone at this bank.

The more they talked, the more we could see that the problem was that she had made a decision without him. He didn't have any real reason not to trust the bank she'd chosen—it was a national branch he'd likely heard of—but he didn't like that she'd gone ahead and deposited a huge amount of their money in a new place without consulting him. It wasn't what she'd done that bothered him. It was that she'd done it without him. And that, for him, felt like financial infidelity.

Her reactions suggested that she was irritated at his seeming lack of trust in her decision. She wanted him to trust her judgment, but he didn't. For her, his need to control her decisions felt like financial infidelity.

We don't have a problem with couples having separate checking accounts. But if you and your spouse have them, take extra care to avoid financial infidelity. These arrangements can be a minefield of mistrust and misunderstanding.

No matter how much money is in your separate accounts, no matter why you have them, it's crucial that you have 100 percent transparency in your communication about those accounts. Both you and your spouse should know exactly how much money is going into those accounts and how much money is going out. As long as you're both fully aware of these accounts and any financial activity they involve, they aren't a problem.

What is a problem is separation for the sake of secrecy or security. If you have a separate credit card because you don't want your spouse to know about it, you're committing financial infidelity. If you have a separate checking account because you don't trust your spouse with your money, you're committing financial infidelity.

We find that every Money Personality can be tempted to keep some money separate from the family finances. Savers want to know they have a little cushion. Spenders like to have a stash that no one else can control. Security Seekers want to protect their nest eggs. Risk Takers want liquid funds they can access quickly. And Flyers don't mean to keep their money separate, but they might forget they still have money in a checking account in the town where they went to college. In other words, all of us can be sucked into financial infidelity.

Maintaining separate finances is like having separate date nights. They might be convenient, but they don't help you grow closer as a couple. They are a sign that there's some trust missing and a lack of partnership. And when there's a lack of trust and cohesiveness in a relationship, financial infidelity is much more likely to worm its way in.

Overspending and Debt

So many couples struggle with spending and debt, especially those of us who are Spenders and Risk Takers. We tend to have a sense of entitlement. We tell ourselves we deserve those golf clubs, that new dress, that boat. We work hard and want to enjoy the fruits of our labors.

But debt can tear a relationship apart. We know couples who, through nothing but a couple of spending sprees, found themselves deep in debt only a few months into their marriages. And once that debt is there, other dreams fly out the door. Buy a house? Forget it—their credit rating is shot. Have a baby? Not in that studio apartment they can barely afford. Change jobs? Go back to school? Travel? Not when every penny they're making is going to the bank.

One couple needed furniture for their first apartment and, in the throes of wedding spending, bought brand-new furniture for their living room (a couch, two chairs, a coffee table, end tables, and lamps), their bedroom (a bed, two dressers, and two nightstands), and dining room (a table, six chairs, and a buffet). When the bill arrived, they were stunned to realize they had accrued several thousand dollars in debt they couldn't pay. They'd figured this was how every couple started out, but a few conversations with friends showed them they had made a very expensive mistake. Ten years into their marriage, they are still paying off that debt, not to mention student loans, car payments, and a few leftover wedding expenses. Their dreams of owning a home have been pushed back and pushed back and pushed back.

The stress of debt can leave couples open to financial infidelity. They agree to cut back, but the Spender can't resist that new video game or those cute shoes.

They are living paycheck to paycheck, but the Risk Taker will use one of those paychecks as an investment in his buddy's new business. And that's when the secrets start; that's when they start lying about their spending, hiding receipts, borrowing money to cover their mistakes. It's an ugly, vicious cycle.

Lack of Planning

We see this come up in older couples we work with, people who are ready to send their kids to college or are nearing retirement. They get to the point where they need a pretty decent chunk of money and they just don't have it.

Remember the story we told you at the beginning of the book about the couple who were getting a divorce after more than forty years of marriage? This was their issue. She was a Security Seeker and he was a Flyer. For years she'd been anxious about their retirement, asking him to put more aside for the future. And he let it go. The closer they got to retirement age, the more anxious she became until she couldn't deal with it anymore and she left him.

Other couples find themselves caught unprepared for the future and get angry at each other. They start blaming each other and trying desperately to solve the problem. One of them might sell off a car or even the house in hopes of bringing in money. The Risk Takers might throw all the couple's life savings into one last-ditch investment in an effort to come up with more money. The Security Seekers will be so freaked out they will shut down emotionally. The whole relationship starts to fall apart from the stress.

Lately, we've been meeting with an increasing number of couples who are struggling to help their kids pay for college. In many cases, they had good intentions to start some sort of savings plan, but those eighteen years fly by and they are caught with a difficult choice: sacrifice their own financial situation to help pay for school, or ask their kids to take out loans that will leave them with huge debt before they have their first job. There is no good solution in these cases, only the lesser of two lousy choices.

The desperation of these situations often leads to plenty of accusations and blame. Carol and Neil will send their oldest daughter off to college in another year, and Carol is panicked. They haven't saved a dime for her education. She and Neil talked about creating a college fund when their daughter was in elementary school, but Neil thought it was pointless. He figured their daughter was going to have to take out loans no matter how much they saved, so they might as well enjoy that money while they had it.

Carol never agreed with this approach, but she didn't want to keep having the same argument, so eventually she stopped bringing it up. But now that their daughter is a junior in high school, she's getting nervous. She had to pay her way through college and it left her with a lot of student loan debt. She doesn't want their daughter to have to deal with that same burden, and she's beyond mad at Neil for never taking this situation seriously.

So now she's taking matters into her own hands. Neil doesn't know it, but she has met with their bank to look into taking out her own loan so she can take on the debt instead. She has looked at the Blue Book value of their cars to see if they could free up some money by selling their vehicles and buying something cheaper. If Neil won't help her, she'll handle it herself.

Now that it's crunch time, Neil feels about the same way he's always felt. He's counting on loans, grants, and work-study to pay for their daughter's college. He doesn't understand why Carol is so worked up about this. He knows plenty of other parents who put their money into retirement instead of college with the idea that it will be easier for their kids to pay off student loans now than have to support their aging parents later. He wants his kids to learn that you have to work for your education—that it means more when they've earned it themselves instead of having it handed to them by their parents.

Neil and Carol are deep in their financial infidelity. The lack of planning ten years ago has led Carol to a state of desperation, one that has all the hallmarks of financial infidelity.

Control

If you have one person in your relationship who controls all the money, we can guarantee there will be financial infidelity in the relationship. We have a client who called one day all fired up. He said, "We need to come in and see you. I just found a $12,000 balance on a credit card that my wife had that I didn't know about. I'm so mad I don't know what to do."

So they came in. He walked in first and his wife walked in behind him. He was all red in the face and she was calm as could be. We sat down and started looking over the credit card bill. As we looked, we didn't see the kinds of expenses we expect to see on a secret credit card—shopping trips, online purchases, travel expenses. Instead, it was trips to the grocery store, household supplies, school supplies.

We asked her to explain the bill to us. She went down the list and said, "That was for extra food for a business dinner we hosted. That was for the kids' school clothes. That was my regular grocery run." There wasn't anything on that bill that shouldn't have been covered by their regular budget. So we asked her why she had a secret card for that stuff. She said, "He doesn't give me enough money to cover these things."

So we turned to our client and said, "This bill isn't her problem. It's your problem. You're controlling the finances so intensely that you don't let her spend what it takes to care for your family."

The more we dug in to this couple's story, the clearer it became that he was a classic controller. He didn't believe she could handle the family finances, so he took care of everything. He didn't trust her to be honest about her spending, so he gave her an allowance that let him keep track of every cent. He didn't talk to her about their money, so he had no idea what it really costs to manage a household.

This is a classic case of one spouse holding the purse strings so tightly that the other spouse is driven to commit financial infidelity by default. When that's happening, it's only a matter of time before that marriage is over. There is no trust, no respect, no partnership. And unless the controlling spouse is willing to let go and build a true Money Relationship, the marriage is done for.

Money Secrets

Money secrets take on a life of their own. One of our favorite stories involves an unintentional money secret. A client of ours told us about something that had happened to him about ten years earlier. He had an opportunity to invest in a company that he was really excited about. He told his wife about it but knew they didn't have the $10,000 he needed to own a share in this business.

His wife looked at him and said, "Wait here." She ran into the bedroom and came back holding a brown grocery bag. She started pulling cash out of the bag—$10, $50, $1,000. She had more than $12,000 in this bag.

He was stunned. "Where did you get this?"

She said, "It's my bra money. My mother taught me this. Every time I go to the store I write a check for $10 extra, put the money in my bra and bring it home. I've been doing it since we got married."

On the one hand, he was thrilled. But he was also a little bothered that they had never talked about it. All that money, for all those years, and he'd never known about it.

In that case, the money secret was a pretty good one. But most of the time, money secrets are disastrous. They bankrupt families and leave a trail of foreclosures, destroyed credit, and deep debt behind them. And, of course, they destroy relationships.

We've told you about some ugly financial infidelity here. And that can make it easy to feel like having a few little secrets now and then is no big deal compared to those couples with years of deception or control behind them. But here's the thing with financial infidelity: even a little bit can create problems in your relationship. Just like a single grain of sand in your shoe can create a painful blister on your foot, a tiny act of financial infidelity can wear away the trust and respect that are crucial to a healthy Money Relationship.

Imagine a glass jar. Every time you commit financial infidelity, no matter how intentional or how innocent, no matter how much or how little money is involved, it's like adding a handful of rocks to that jar. Every handful crowds out the good stuff that makes a marriage work.

The good news is that you can overcome financial infidelity. You can stop it, right now, and move forward by forgiving each other and building new patterns in your Money Relationship. In the next chapter, we're going to teach you how to dump all those rocks of resentment and anger and mistrust and control and replace them with communication and cooperation.

MAKE IT HAPPEN

Identify one of the five causes of financial infidelity that you've seen in your marriage. Now make one commitment that can help you end that financial infidelity. For example, you can decide to talk about any purchase over $100 or agree to look over credit card statements together every month.

9

The Money Dump

How are you doing? We know that those last couple of chapters might have been painful, especially if you have a lot of financial infidelity in your relationship. So before we move on, we want to remind you of that commitment you made at the very beginning of the book. You believed you had a relationship worth saving. And that belief makes all the difference.

We know that not every relationship can survive lies and secrets and years of resentment. But we also know that when couples are willing to try something new, to break out of old patterns and learn new skills, they can rebuild their marriages. And that's what the next few chapters are about. We're going to give you three tools that you can use from here on out to get your Money Relationship back on track and start living out those dreams you had when you met.

A strong Money Relationship doesn't just happen. It takes some work, but we think the work can be kind of fun. We've designed these three tools—the Money Dump, the Money Huddle, and the Stop, Drop, and Roll Guide to Fighting Fair—to be easy to remember and easy to fit into your busy lives. We've also designed them to bring you closer together as a couple by showing you how to communicate about money in honest, respectful ways.

Before we launch into the Money Dump, however, we want to do a quick recap. Everything you've learned so far is going to come into play as you learn how to use these three tools. Your Money Personality, the Opposite Dynamic, your partner's Money Personality, and financial infidelity will all come into play as you unpack the issues you're dealing with as a couple and figure out what to do about them.

So take a minute to think about your Money Personalities, your spouse's Money Personalities, and the challenges and opportunities they create when they come together. Then think about those areas of financial infidelity you identified in the previous chapters. Consider how your Money Personalities have played into that financial infidelity.

Now you're ready for the Money Dump.

Getting It All Out

When Bethany was growing up, her family took in foster children. There was one girl in particular who drove Bethany crazy—and vice versa. Finally, Bethany's mother got tired of the constant tension between the girls and came up with a brilliant solution. She had each of them write down every-thing about the other one that bugged her. Then, each had to write down everything she appreciated about the other. And that was it.

For Bethany, the act of writing the list was enough to release some of the tension she felt with her foster sister. It helped just to dump it all out on a piece of paper, even if nothing between them actually changed.

That's what the Money Dump is all about. It's a chance for you to dump out all the fears and worries and hopes you have for your Money Relationship. It's *not* the time to rip into your spouse or make a list of all her wrongdoings. You're not dumping *on* your spouse. You're dumping all the emotional crud inside you that is holding you back from really working *with* your spouse.

The Money Dump is also a way to celebrate the victories in your Money Relationship, no matter how insignificant they might seem. It's a way to name what's working so you can capitalize on your strengths. It's a way to show your spouse that you notice the contributions she makes to the family. It's a way to talk about what's really happening in your Money Relationship.

Here's how it works.

$\Big($ **For more "The Dump" resources, go to TheMoneyCouple.com.** $\Big)$

The Money Dump

Step 1: Be Alone

Start in separate rooms. Get a piece of paper and a pencil and find a quiet spot to do your Money Dump. Being alone lets you get rid of any distractions so you can really focus. And being alone helps you be more honest. You aren't going to share everything on your list with your partner, so you have nothing to lose by being completely vulnerable in your lists. Find your own space and let the words fly.

Step 2: Pros and Cons

Make a line down the paper, dividing it into two columns. In one column, write out all the pros of your Money Relationship: What are you grateful for? What gives you hope? What's working? What do you appreciate about your spouse? About yourself? How are your Money Personalities helping you reach your dreams? What are those dreams? How do you feel about your FRI score? In the other column, list your cons. Remember, this isn't meant to become a list of all the ways your spouse has messed up your finances. It's a way to lay out all stressors, the fears, the challenges you see in your Money Relationship.

Here's what our friend Hannah's list looked like:

PROS	CONS
We have a house.	We never do anything fun because it costs too much.
We have jobs.	I feel like I can't spend money without Jerry's permission.
We have a little money in savings.	I hate my job but can't afford to quit.
We are good at buying things on sale.	Our mortgage is too high.
We don't go out much, so that saves money.	We don't have enough saved for retirement and time's running out.
Jerry is good with money.	We haven't gone on vacation in five years.
We paid off our student loans.	Jerry works too much overtime.
We don't have much debt except our mortgage and a car payment.	We fight about money a lot.

PROS	CONS
We can usually buy the kids the things they need for school.	We have the Opposite Dynamic.
I'm a good bargain hunter.	I want to help my parents out but we can't afford it.
We know our Money Personalities: I'm a Saver/Security Seeker; Jerry is a Saver/Flyer.	I get stressed out during the holidays and birthdays because I hate spending money on gifts people don't need.
We don't have a lot of financial infidelity.	
We trust each other.	

Step 3: Circle One Con

Choose the one con that's creating the most tension in your relationship. If there's an issue that's been bugging you and you just haven't known how to bring it up, this is your chance. You'll be sharing this con with your spouse, so make sure you find a way to talk about it that doesn't place all the blame at your spouse's feet.

Here's Hannah's con:

We don't have enough
saved for retirement and
time's running out.

We haven't gone on
vacation in five years.

Jerry works too much
overtime.

Step 4: Get Together

Sit down at the kitchen table or on the living room couch
and look each other in the eyes. You are doing something *so*
important for your relationship, and we want you to take a
moment to look at each other and remember that you are in
this together.

Step 5: Read Your List of Pros Out Loud

When we do the Money Dump with couples, we love
watching this process unfold. There was a couple, Dan and
Julie, who barely looked at each other when they arrived at
the seminar. When we worked through the Money Dump
with them, we weren't sure what to expect. They were having a hard time coming up with pros, so we suggested they

start each item with the words "I appreciate that . . .". So Julie started reading her list of pros. She said, "I appreciate that you work so hard for our family." And as soon as she said it, some of the tension went out of his shoulders. You could see his defenses going down.

Then it was his turn. He said, "I appreciate that you clip coupons."

She looked stunned and said, "I thought you hated that."

He looked at her and responded, "I never said that."

Her shoulders softened as she said, "You're right; you didn't."

They hadn't changed any behaviors yet, but they saw each other differently. They saw what was real in their Money Relationship—a sense of mutual respect and recognition. That simple conversation breathed life back into their relationship. For the rest of the seminar, they looked at each other, talked, even laughed as though they were getting to know each other for the first time.

Step 6: Share Your One Con

Just one. One. Only one. One. We've found that in a lot of cases, both spouses have the same con. Even if you don't, you'll probably find that you have similar ideas about what you want to work on in your Money Relationship. Do your best during this step to stick with your own feelings about the situation you're discussing. Nothing good will come from blaming the other person. So if you're concerned that your spouse is spending too much, explain why that concerns you—"I'm worried we won't have any money for retirement and I really want to travel with you someday." Or, "I'd love to spend our money on things that really matter to us."

Step 7: Commit for Ninety Days

Commit to working on both of your cons for the next ninety days. They might not get solved, but you'll be working on them together. In the next two chapters we'll explain the Money Huddle—a regular time to get together and work out a plan for dealing with these cons. So for now, just figure out what you want to work on. That's it. It might not seem like much, but think about it like this: until you started reading this book, you weren't doing anything to improve your Money Relationship. If this is the only thing you do after reading this book, you'll have improved your relationship by leaps and bounds.

We suggest doing a Money Dump once a year. That's it. Just once a year. In between, keep track of your cons and celebrate your progress, even when it's just a little step in the right direction. And keep thinking up pros to add to next year's list. You'll be surprised at how quickly that list grows.

In the next two chapters we're going to show you how to use the Money Huddle to keep the momentum going.

MAKE IT HAPPEN

Okay, go ahead and do your Money Dump.

Really. You're ready. Good luck!

10

The Money Huddle

The Money Dump is a turning point for a lot of couples. For many of them, it's the first time they've gotten all these feelings about their Money Relationship out. It's the first time they've taken an honest look at what's working. And that feels really good.

There's something cathartic about getting all that crud out of your system, but if you stop there, you're missing out on the best part of rebuilding your Money Relationship. That happens in the Money Huddle.

A Money Huddle is a time you and your spouse set aside to talk about your Money Relationship. In the next chapter we'll give you an easy outline to guide you through your Money Huddle. But before we do that, we want to help you understand what this little sit-down is really about.

Being Intentional

The vast majority of the couples we meet are consumed by worry. They are worried about their debt. They are worried about their savings. They're worried about the future. And that worry is a big reason why their Money Relationships are a mess. They are so stressed out that even those little decisions about where to eat dinner or what kind of coffee to buy turn into major fights.

They think all that worry and stress is about their budget. But it's not. It's about their Money Relationships. No matter how much debt you have or how little money you have saved up, you can have a strong, healthy Money Relationship. But you have to know how to separate the details of your budget from the details of your Money Relationship.

By now you've read enough that you know the difference between your finances and your Money Relationship. Remember Jonell and Kai? We told you all about their income and expenses and debt. That was their financial situation. It was *not* their Money Relationship. Now *you're* going to be intentional about separating your financial situation from your Money Relationship. And you're going to do that by using the Money Huddle.

The Money Huddle is not the time to balance your checkbook or pay your bills. It's not the time to gripe at your spouse about how much he spent getting the car detailed or blame your spouse for not keeping all of her receipts. It's not the time to look over your retirement plans or talk through potential investments. In other words, the Money Huddle is not the time to deal with your financial situation.

Instead, the Money Huddle is a time to reconnect, to build trust, to work together to assess the present and dream about the future.

It would be great if conversations like this just happened spontaneously. But for most of us, there just isn't time to focus on the emotional side of our Money Relationships. So instead we yell or blame or get irritated and stew. And that's how our Money Relationships get off track.

You've done a lot of hard work to get this far. Now it's time to take advantage of how far you've come and keep moving forward. When you set aside time each month to talk through the realities of your financial situation, to tell your spouse what you need in your Money Relationship, and to dream about the future together, you can put an end to fights, stop blaming each other, and grow closer than you've been in a long time.

The Money Huddle Defined

When we talk with couples about the Money Huddle, they assume it's a time to do their family bookkeeping together. It's not. We're going to repeat ourselves here to make sure there's no confusion. There's a practical side to your Money Relationship—managing your money, balancing the books, paying the bills. But for so many couples, their understanding of the Money Relationship stops there. They don't realize that the Money Relationship is really about the emotional side of your money decisions. But your budget and your Money Relationship are not the same thing. So we've pulled the practical side and the emotional side apart to make that distinction clear and to help you really focus on the emotional aspect of your Money Relationship.

There are four reasons why we want you to keep the practical side and the emotional side of your Money Relationship separate.

1. IT KEEPS IT FROM FEELING LIKE A MEETING. In most relationships, there is a "money person," the one who balances the checkbook and pays the bills. If your Money Huddle is all about the practical side of your Money Relationship, it's a fairly one-sided affair. It just isn't feasible or enjoyable for most couples to pay their bills together. So let the money person take care of that. Your Money Huddle will be a major failure if it boils down to one person holding a meeting while the other one just listens. Instead, this is a time for compromise, mutual respect, and joint decision making. It's a time to look ahead together.

2. IT DEFUSES THE TENSION. Most of us get a little anxious when we're paying bills and looking over our

accounts. So it's not the best time to bring up plans or needs or ideas about how you can strengthen your communication. Having a separate Money Huddle gives you a little emotional distance from the immediate demands of your finances.

3. IT PUTS THE FOCUS ON YOUR RELATIONSHIP. If the only time you talk about your Money Relationship is when you're paying bills, it's easy to think your budget is the defining factor in your relationship. But it's not. What matters are your Money Personalities, the impact of the Opposite Dynamic, and the financial infidelity that threatens to creep into your relationship. What matters is how you work together to make those never-ending decisions that involve money. Having a separate Money Huddle gives you the time and mental space you need to deal with those issues well.

4. IT KEEPS YOU CLOSE AND CONNECTED. It might be hard to imagine right now, but we promise that if you stay committed to a monthly Money Huddle and use that time to talk through your Money Relationship, you will reclaim the intimacy you want in your marriage. You will find ways to keep money from tearing you apart and instead allow your Money Relationship to draw you together in ways you've only dreamed about.

Not long ago, we had a couple come into our office. They arrived in separate cars and hardly looked at each other while we talked with them. We asked them to commit to a Money Dump and at least one Money Huddle. They agreed and left the office looking as miserable as they had when they'd come in.

But a month later, they came back. They held hands while they sat in the waiting room. They laughed together when they told us how they'd stumbled through their first Money Huddle. They finished each other's sentences as they told us about the dreams they came up with during their Money Huddle. They walked out of the office smiling at each other and exchanged a kiss or two before getting in the car together and heading home. You might have a slightly longer road to smooching it up in front of your financial planner, but we're confident that if you commit to these regular, focused, honest times of conversation, you're going to grow closer.

We know that, for a lot of couples, the idea of adding one more commitment to an already overloaded life feels like too much to ask. So we've kept the Money Huddle simple. It's forty-five minutes, once a month. In the next chapter, we'll lay out exactly how you'll use that forty-five minutes. If you think of this as an investment in your relationship, a chance to reclaim the life you used to dream about, then that seems like a pretty reasonable price to pay.

MAKE IT HAPPEN

Take some time to discuss together what you
are looking forward to and what fears you
have about doing a Money Huddle together.

11

Begin with the E.N.D.

In his bestselling book *The 7 Habits of Highly Effective People*, Stephen Covey suggests that those who want to be successful in life should "begin with the end in mind."[1] That's certainly true when it comes to your Money Relationship.

You need to have a vision for what your Money Relationship could look like. We find that most couples have a fairly simple vision. They want to stop fighting. They want a Money Relationship in which they work together instead of battling each other. They want to make decisions without arguing and solve problems without blame. They want harmony instead of conflict. So what do you want?

Think about that question for a minute. What do you want your Money Relationship to be like? Do you want to be

---

1. Stephen Covey, *The 7 Habits of Highly Effective People* (New York: Simon & Schuster, 1989).

equal partners in making financial decisions or are you okay with having a "money person"? Can you accept the occasional argument as long as it doesn't get nasty and personal? Are you willing to cut back on spending or reduce your savings in order to have a more peaceful Money Relationship? If you come to your first Money Huddle with a clear vision for the future, you're going to have a much easier time listening to each other and being willing to compromise than if you just show up and expect your problems to take care of themselves.

This is where your Money Dump will come in handy. Remember the cons you identified? They can be your guide to creating a vision for your Money Relationship.

In the previous chapter, Hannah's con was that she and her husband, Jerry, hadn't gone on vacation in five years. That's a big con. So for Hannah, a healthy Money Relationship is one that balances security and savings with regular doses of fun, rest, and time with Jerry. That's a clear, doable goal, one Jerry can sign on to as well.

Once you have a vision for your Money Relationship, you have to be intentional about making that vision a reality. You have to be committed to developing new patterns of communication. You have to be willing to give up some long-standing habits. And you have to be willing to set aside forty-five minutes a month to talk about your Money Relationship.

The E.N.D.

We use the acronym E.N.D. to help you keep your Money Huddle focused. The fastest way to kill the momentum you have right now is to turn your Money Huddle into a two-hour gripe-fest or let it flip over into a conversation about the details of your finances. Instead, keep your time short and to the point. Your forty-five minutes will be broken into three fifteen-minute chunks, each of them focused on one task.

Evaluate

Use the first fifteen minutes of your Money Huddle to evaluate your current financial situation. We know, we just said this wasn't the time to talk about your financial situation. But we also want you to deal with the real story of your financial life as you work on your Money Relationship. So keep your conversation limited to the two biggest issues in your finances—debt and savings. We can't stress how important it is to stick with these two topics and nothing else! These are the areas that create the most tension in a relationship; most of us have too much of one and not enough of the other. You're not going to discuss every expense or deposit—you can do that later. You're just getting a general overview of where you are right now. There should be two numbers to review: how much debt you have and how much you have in savings. Two numbers; that's it.

This step is simple, but it's the key to putting an end to financial infidelity. Financial infidelity thrives on secrets. It feeds off of a spouse's willingness to be in the dark about the realities of a couple's money. This step shines a light on what's real—no more secrets, no more ignorance, no more hiding. When you know what's real in your financial picture, you can start making plans. You can move forward. You can get rid of the fear and anxiety and mistrust and start over.

This is where the money person in the relationship gets to report on what's happening with the family savings and debt. But that person doesn't get to dominate the conversation. Her job is to lay out the facts, then spend the rest of the fifteen minutes working with her spouse to make plans for reducing that debt or increasing that savings.

Start with your savings—all of it. What do you have in your retirement account? How about the kids' college fund? What do you have for emergency funds or vacation funds or let's-buy-a-house funds? Lay it all out and talk about where you are. Talk very generally about where you would like to see more savings and where you might be saving too much. What kind of realistic changes can you make that will get you where you want to go? If you're not sure where to start, we have all kinds of planning tools on our website, TheMoneyCouple.com, to get you started.

Then do the same thing with your debt. Look at your

car payments, your mortgage, any loans you have, any personal debt you owe. As you do, remember that your debt isn't the issue—you can get yourselves out of debt. What's really important is that you communicate, that you work together to come up with solutions, and that you move forward instead of look back.

One more word about debt: we know a lot of financial advisors who put the fear of God into people about debt. They treat it as though it's the child of the devil himself. And while debt can indeed be devastating, it is not the real problem for most couples.

We've been deep, deep in debt in our marriage. Like $50,000 deep. And it was scary. It took us a long time to claw our way out of it. But our debt didn't tear us apart. In some ways, it made us closer. We had to work really hard to get out of debt, but we were working together. We talked about it. We made a plan and we stuck with it. When we stumbled, we pulled each other back up and kept climbing. And we didn't dwell on the reasons we had accumulated that debt. We just looked ahead and rebuilt our finances. And along the way, we made our marriage even stronger. Now we look back on that experience with a little pride; we overcame something big and we did it as partners. That feels really good.

But we know couples who have called it quits over one-tenth of our debt. That's because the debt isn't their real issue; it's the Money Relationship that's broken, not the bank account.

If you have debt, don't beat yourselves up over it. It's just how life works sometimes, and there's nothing to be gained by feeling ashamed or guilty about being in debt. Those feelings can quickly spiral into inaction, blame, and more financial infidelity. So stop listening to that voice that tells you debt is from the devil. It's not. It's just debt.

Whether you are $5,000 or $50,000 in debt, we want you to face the realities of your financial situation together. We want you to figure out how to deal with that situation together. We want you to see yourselves as true partners as you move forward together.

The *Evaluate* part of your Money Huddle might be a little painful the first time you work through it. If you've had years of financial infidelity in your Money Relationship, you'll have all kinds of secrets to untangle. But you don't have to deal with all of it at once. Take it one Money Huddle at a time and you can get through this. Do everything in your power to resist blaming each other and focus on how you can fix it. You have made a fresh start, and this process is only going to get easier.

Needs

The next fifteen minutes of your Money Huddle is the time to talk about what you need in your Money Relationship.

Most of us are terrible at telling other people what we need, especially when it comes to money. We assume our spouses know that we have a hunting weekend planned for the same weekend every year or that we need a new outfit for a big presentation at work. They might know, but clear communication never hurts.

This is the time to keep everything you've learned about your Money Personalities in the forefront. If your spouse is a Security Seeker and he tells you he needs the family to cut back on spending, you know it's not because he's trying to be controlling; it's because he's worried. So talk about his anxiety. What does he need in order to feel secure? If you're a Spender and you're feeling the pinch of a tighter budget, talk about your need to have some freedom in your spending. Can you set up a small "mad money" fund that gives you a little leeway without busting the budget?

This is also the time to look at the cons you chose during your Money Dump. Those cons are really needs in disguise. So talk about what you need to get that con off your list. If it's a vacation, say so—and start planning. If it's more trust, say so and make it happen.

By being honest about your needs, you show your spouse that you trust her, that you value her insight, and that you believe the two of you can work together to solve problems. That kind of affirmation goes a long way toward connecting you as a couple.

Dream

The final fifteen-minute segment of the Money Huddle is our favorite. This is when you're going to grab your dreams again and put together a plan for making them happen. It's a monthly deposit in your Money Relationship that will add up quickly.

We see it over and over again. When couples dream together, they move forward together. And when they stop dreaming, they stop growing as a couple. So take this time each month to envision the future you want to build together.

During one of our Money Huddles, we started talking about our retirement. We love to travel, but we wanted to do something different when we retired. So we came up with an idea. We're going to spend a year living in four different cities around the world. We'll each pick two and spend three months in each city.

We know it's kind of a strange dream, but it suits us. And once we came up with the idea, we started putting money into our retirement fund to make it a reality one day. That dream is helping us keep our savings on track. Because we are dreaming about the same thing, we're working together to make that dream happen.

This is the time to talk about short-term dreams and long-term dreams, personal dreams and dreams for your family. Nothing is off-limits. Maybe you want to take a pottery class— talk about it and figure out how to make it happen. Maybe you want to help your aging parents with their health-care costs. Maybe you want to stay home with your kids or start a new job or move into a different house. Maybe you want to give more to your church or to a charity that's important to you. You had these dreams before and you can get them back.

Whatever your dreams are, talk about them and start planning for them. We suggest couples bring a calendar to their Money Huddles. The process of dreaming together will draw you closer and build a deeper sense of connection and intimacy.

The Money Huddle brings together all the skills and knowledge you've developed while reading this book. And as the months go by and you stay committed to monthly Money Huddles, you'll see your Money Relationship change dramatically. You'll put an end to constant battles, mistrust, resentment, and financial infidelity, and you'll replace them with meaningful conversations about your life together. And that's worth more than the fattest bank account.

Something else happens when you use this time to talk about what you need from your Money Relationship. You'll actually stop talking about money all the time. When you know you have a time set aside to deal with issues that come up during the month, you'll find that you don't talk about them over every meal or as you're getting ready for bed. And when you're not talking about money all the time, you suddenly have time to talk about other things.

We worked with a couple not long ago. He was a Flyer/ Spender; she was a Security Seeker/Saver. You know enough about Money Personalities now to recognize that this relationship could have been a disaster. It wasn't . . . yet. But there were signs that it was heading that way. He spent money they didn't have; she was freaking out. Same song, second verse.

We encouraged them to try holding regular Money Huddles and report back to us in a couple of months. Sure enough, they came back with a renewed commitment to make their marriage work. The Money Huddles, they said, had been a great tool for helping them manage the way they talked about money. For a long time, he'd been frustrated that all of their conversations seemed to eventually come back to his spending. She was frustrated that he didn't seem to listen to her requests that he spend less.

But the Money Huddle gave them a forum for talking about these issues in a calm way rather than in the heat of a disagreement. When their daily conversations started to turn into money conversations, he could ask her to table that concern and bring it up in their Money Huddle. And during the Money Huddle, he was more inclined to listen to her concerns and work with her to figure out some compromises in his spending habits. She felt heard, he felt that the nagging had stopped, and they could both see that their Money Relationship was improving.

MAKE IT HAPPEN

Plan your first Money Huddle. Really. Right now. Go get your spouse and your calendar and find forty-five minutes to start your new Money Relationship with the E.N.D. in mind.

PART 3

. . .

Reclaiming
Your Marriage

12

Why We Fight

It might seem strange to talk about fighting when we've just taken you through the Money Huddle lovefest. But here's the thing: no matter how great you get at communicating, no matter how well you understand each other's Money Personalities, no matter how many dreams you work toward, you're still going to fight about money.

The tools we've given you aren't magic. They aren't going to make you suddenly agree on every money decision. They will dramatically reduce the number of arguments you have about money, but they won't prevent you from ever having a heated conversation over your finances. We know because we still have those fights ourselves.

In the next chapter, we'll show you how to keep those fights from escalating into hurtful arguments that leave permanent emotional scars. But first, we want to show you why fights about money can be so painful and damaging to a relationship.

Hitting the Core

We had a couple in our office a few years ago who had been married for about five years. He'd grown up with a lot of money and she'd grown up with very little. He was a Saver, she was a Spender, and the Opposite Dynamic was a major factor in their relationship. It didn't take long for their conversation to turn into a screaming match. We could tell this was an old fight, one they'd come back to over and over.

The fundamental issue between them was that she was spending more than he thought she should. They fought about what she spent and where she spent it. After listening for a few minutes, we stopped them and said, "Hang on. Let's get to the heart of this problem. Why do you keep spending when he's asking you not to? Why won't you stick to the budget?"

She said, "My parents were missionaries and I grew up dirt-poor. We had two meals a day if we were lucky. Sometimes we didn't have toilet paper. My husband makes a great living and I don't see why he won't let me spend money. I deserve to have nice things after spending so much of my life with nothing."

He looked at her like he'd never heard this before.

Then we turned to him and gave him a chance to speak his piece. He looked at his wife and said, "I don't trust you with our money. I'm afraid you're going to bankrupt us and we won't have a future if you keep spending like this."

And her jaw hit the ground.

They both realized that the other person had deep-seated needs that weren't being met in their Money Relationship, needs that were part of their very different Money Personalities. And those differences had led to intense arguments that had left both of them emotionally bruised.

Arguments about money hurt us like very few other fights do. They feel intensely personal. We feel attacked and get defensive. We walk away from them filled with anger, resentment, and a deep sense of mistrust. For a long time, we didn't understand why money fights seemed to create such complex, long-term problems for couples. But when we thought about how deeply embedded our Money Personalities are, it all started to make sense.

So often, money fights are the result of our differing perspectives on money. We look at the way the other person makes decisions and we just don't get it. So we criticize and blame and attack. And that's why money fights hurt so much. Our Money Personalities are so deeply personal, so central to who we are, that to insult them is to insult us at our core. It doesn't feel as if your spouse is criticizing your actions; it feels as if he or she is criticizing who you are.

Which is exactly what he or she is doing. Your Money

Personality is as much a part of you as your eye color or the size of your feet. And you have as much chance of changing it as you do making your feet two sizes bigger.

Most of us are fairly aware of our flaws. You know if you have a tendency to be impatient or irritable, if you have a short fuse or procrastinate. While we don't like hearing other people name our faults, we know they're right when they do it. But we tend to really like our own Money Personalities. We see them as a great way to approach financial decisions. So when someone we love tells us that approach is stupid or irrational or crazy, it feels very different from someone pointing out our flaws. It feels as if they are attacking the good parts of who we are, not the parts that need work. And when we believe we've been acting in the best interest of our families, it hurts even more for our spouses to come along and tell us all the reasons we're failing them.

Cal is a Saver's Saver. His friends tell him he's cheap, and he laughs it off because he knows it's true. He prides himself on getting a lot for a little, on living on next to nothing, and on making his way on his own with no help from anyone. He paid his way through college by working three jobs and living for free with a couple he met through his church. Sure, he slept on a cot in their unfinished basement—not exactly a comfy apartment—but he didn't care. Free was free. He could feed himself for a week on one of those rotisserie chickens from the grocery store. His entire wardrobe was made up of stuff from the thrift store and castoffs from the older son of the couple he lived with.

Believe it or not, Cal found a woman who didn't mind his Saver ways. Well, not at first. In the early days of their relationship, Carmen thought Cal was charming. She loved how nonmaterialistic he was, how free-spirited and unconcerned with status he seemed to be. He would make her funky little gifts out of old magazines or cereal boxes, and she thought they were the most wonderful things she'd ever seen.

But after a few years of marriage, Cal's thrifty ways started to lose their charm. Cal was a social studies teacher at the middle school in town and Carmen was a nurse. Together, they made a reasonable living, enough to afford a little house and two used cars. They eventually had a couple of children and a lovely life together.

But Cal never let go of his saving ways. Even when they could afford to do otherwise, he insisted they wash out their plastic bags and reuse aluminum foil. He wore his socks until they had holes in the heels and the toes and refused to let Carmen buy him new pants, even when his trusty khakis were worn almost bare in the knees.

Most frustrating for Carmen was Cal's unwillingness to buy her something nice for her birthday, their anniversary, or Christmas. She still loved the sweet homemade cards he gave her, but part of her really wanted some killer earrings, just once. She had come right out and told him so more than once—and still, nothing. For Carmen, Cal's unwillingness to spend money on her felt like he was more concerned about saving money than he was about her feelings.

On her most recent birthday, Carmen reached the limits of her patience. She opened her card and asked if Cal had gotten her a gift. Before he could answer, she looked at him and said sarcastically, "Wait, let me guess. You made me a diamond necklace out of tin foil and a paper clip. Gee, I'm so glad you didn't have to spend any money on me."

Cal was stunned. She'd always liked his little homemade cards and gifts. Why was she so angry? He made the mistake of asking her, and that's when it all came out. Years of feeling slighted by her husband's thrifty ways came pouring out of Carmen. She told him he was stingy, cheap, and selfish. And Cal was crushed.

From Cal's perspective, it was his willingness to do without that helped him get where he was. He drove an old car and saved every penny he could so that they could afford a nice house. He never asked for Christmas gifts because he wanted to make sure they could afford something nice for their kids. He never bought new clothes because he wanted to make sure they'd be able to send the kids to college. In his mind, it was his "cheapness" that allowed them to live so well. Carmen's words hit Cal right in the gut. It would take a lot of work to repair the relational damage those words created.

If you and your spouse want to prevent money arguments from reaching that hurtful level, you have to respect each other's Money Personalities and avoid making them the center of your conflicts.

Behind the Conflict

Our Money Personalities aren't the cause of money fights, but unless we are aware of how our Money Personalities influence our outlook on money, we can fall into some bad habits that can lead to terrible conflict.

In our years of working with couples, we've seen three main causes behind money fights.

We Don't Own Our Money Personalities

Your Money Personality can be awesome. It can lead you to great wealth; it can keep you from ending up deep in debt; it can help you provide for your family; it can inspire you to acts of tremendous generosity. But every Money Personality has its challenges. And we ignore those challenges at our own risk.

So many of the arguments we see are the result of one or both spouses ignoring the downside of their Money

Personalities. We know Spenders who refuse to acknowledge their impulsivity. We know Savers who are downright stingy and proud of it. That failure to own up to the challenges of their Money Personalities makes these people incredibly hard to work with, let alone live with.

If you really want to stop arguing about money all the time, you have to be willing to own your Money Personalities—the good and the not-so-good. You have to be humble enough to see where you've contributed to the broken Money Relationship and strong enough to change your ways, or at least admit change is needed.

We Act Out of Selfishness

Almost all of the financial infidelity we see is the result of (at least) one spouse's selfishness. When they get caught, they have nothing but excuses:

- "I was afraid we were going to lose all our money on your business deal, so I kept some cash for myself."
- "I wanted to be able to shop when I wanted to, so I opened up my own credit card."
- "I really wanted that new car, so I drained our kids' college accounts."
- "I like to go out to eat, so if you don't want to I'll go out with friends instead."

Anytime we keep the focus on ourselves and what we want, no matter what it costs us in relationship capital, we're asking for a fight. It's hard to blame someone for getting angry when his spouse has acted in a way that completely disregards who he is or what he wants.

If you have a history of financial infidelity in your Money Relationship, this is the time to end it for good. It won't be easy. You'll have to keep reminding yourself not to make false assumptions about your spouse. You'll have to risk trusting her even if you've been burned in the past. You'll have to be willing to give up what you want for the sake of your relationship. And the only one who can make that stick is you.

We Get Money Grumpy

Our Money Personalities give us a kind of personal comfort zone. And we like it there. Spenders like being in stores with total purchasing power. Put a Spender on a tight budget and she's going to get grumpy. Savers hate to shop. Take a Saver on a shopping spree and he's going to get grumpy.

It might sound silly to talk about a grumpy Saver, but when we are pushed out of our comfort zones, we act like animals who have been torn from their natural habitat. We get aggressive. We get defensive. We get protective of our needs. And that leads to arguments.

You probably have plenty of stories of your own to prove

this point. Nearly every money conflict has some element of the money grumps in it. You come home from the store and your Security Seeker spouse wants to see your receipt. You feel defensive; she feels anxious. And bam! Before you know it, that shopping trip has sparked a shouting match.

You can't avoid getting money grumpy. Sooner or later you're going to be forced out of your Money Personality comfort zone. But you can change how you react to the perceived threat. Instead of getting defensive or anxious or protective, figure out how to be yourself in that situation. If you're a Spender with a budget, challenge yourself to do more with less. If you're a Saver tagging along on a shopping spree, see what kind of deals you can find. Get comfortable in your own skin and you'll find you don't need to react and get grumpy. You can take whatever comes and make it work for you.

You've done great work so far. And even with all the new information and tools you have, you are still two people with two different perspectives on money. You are going to make decisions your spouse doesn't understand. And your spouse is going to make decisions you don't understand. But when you feel close to your spouse, when you know you have shared goals and dreams for your future, then you don't want to hurt each other. And when you do, you want to make it right. That's what happens when your Money Relationship is working.

MAKE IT HAPPEN

It's hard to stop fighting when all you can see is the negative side of your spouse. So try to change your view. Make an appreciation list for your spouse. Write down three or four aspects of your spouse's Money Personality that are making a positive difference in your Money Relationship. Then share your list.

13

How to Fight Fair

We know a man who is a professional athlete. A few years ago, he signed with a new team in a different part of the country. While he was meeting with his new team and signing his contract, he decided to do a little house hunting. By the end of the day, not only had he found a great house for his family, he'd bought it!

He called his wife from the hotel later that night to tell her the good news. And she was livid.

Now if you're a Spender, a Risk Taker, or a Flyer, you might wonder why she got so upset. He had nothing but good intentions and was doing what he thought was best for his family.

If you're a Saver or a Security Seeker, however, you probably got nervous just reading that story. The idea of your spouse spending that kind of money without your input feels like the worst kind of betrayal.

It took years for our friend and his wife to recover from this incident. She didn't trust him; he felt that she didn't respect him. It was a long, ugly fight that ran like a current under their relationship for a long, long time.

No matter what your Money Personalities, no matter what your past looks like, no matter how committed you are to building a better future, you are going to have disagreements about money. But what you do with those disagreements, well, that's what separates the average marriage from a great marriage.

The Rules of Engagement

Remember those fire safety demonstrations you saw in elementary school? The nice firefighters would visit the school and talk about smoke detectors and escape routes and all those other ways of staying safe in case of a fire. But the one we all know by heart is what you're supposed to do if you're on fire: Stop, Drop, and Roll.

Stop, Drop, and Roll is good advice for putting out emotional fires too. Here's how it works.

Stop

Let's say your spouse comes home from running errands one Saturday and pulls a nice new pair of skis out of the back of the van. The old you might have stood in the doorway with that look of disapproval clouding your face, just daring your spouse to bring them in the house. And when he did, well, then the sparks would fly. "What on earth did you do? We can't afford those! What were you thinking?" In a matter of minutes, you're in the thick of a hurtful fight.

But what if you stopped? What if you didn't say anything about the skis in the heat of the moment and let yourself settle down for a bit first? Instead of yelling at your spouse or accusing him of being an idiot, imagine what would happen if you just told him how you felt. You might say, "Honey, I thought we'd agreed we would talk about any purchases over $50. Can you help me understand why you bought these skis without talking to me about it?"

Not only is the whole tone of that statement less accusatory, but it leaves room for your spouse to either offer a good explanation—"They were on clearance for $25 and I thought we could use them as a Christmas gift for my sister"—or admit his mistake and find a way to make it right—"I guess I got carried away at the store and forgot about our agreement. I'm sorry. I'll return them this afternoon."

The simple act of stopping yourself from reacting out of anger can defuse a potentially explosive argument before it starts. That doesn't mean you never speak up; you have every right to advocate for your needs. But it does give you time to simmer down and think about what's really behind your reaction—fear, worry, mistrust, a sense of disrespect—so you can talk about that feeling instead of the money. *Because it's not about the money.*

Drop

They say that assumptions are the lowest form of knowledge. That's certainly true in a Money Relationship. That's why the second rule to remember is to drop your assumptions.

The vast majority of money fights start with assumptions. You assume your spouse was dishonest when she failed to mention the $40 she spent on lunch with friends when the truth is that she's a Flyer who didn't think it was worth mentioning. You assume your spouse is being controlling about your spending when in reality she's been trying to limit the family expenses so you can all take a vacation this winter.

A few years ago, Bethany came home from work to find an e-mail from a ski school at one of our favorite Colorado ski areas. The e-mail included an itemized list of the costs of ski lessons for our two sons. Now, we had talked about signing them up for ski lessons, but we hadn't agreed to do it yet. So when Bethany saw this e-mail, her first reaction was to assume that I'd gone ahead and signed them up for $800 worth of lessons. She was not happy.

Later, Bethany told me she had the phone in her hand, ready to call me at work and bawl me out for making such a huge decision without her. Those ski lessons violated every agreement we had about how we handle our money. But she didn't call me. She put the phone down, took a deep breath, and decided to wait until I got home so we could talk about it in person.

By the time I got home, Bethany had reread the e-mail and realized it wasn't a bill but an estimate, one I had requested, even though I knew it was going to be far too expensive for us to consider. She asked me about it and I told her about the aggressive sales guy at the ski school who insisted on sending me more information even after I'd told him we weren't interested.

And then we ate dinner.

Imagine what that day might have looked like if Bethany hadn't dropped her assumptions and taken a look at the reality of the situation. She would have called me in the middle of my workday, furious at me. I would have been ticked off that she'd accused me of sneaking that much money by her. I would have spent the rest of the day fuming and she would have done the same. Eventually we would have figured out what really happened, but by then the damage would have been done. Instead of a nice little anecdote, we'd have a painful memory of a terrible fight.

Dropping your assumptions allows you to see what's real in a situation. And when you see what's real, you can deal with it calmly. You can ask questions, talk about what went wrong, and find a solution. You can't do any of that when you're basing everything on an assumption.

Roll

The final rule for fighting fair is to roll up your sleeves and find a way to work together. When it comes to resolving money conflicts, there is no substitute for compromise and cooperation. In one of our previous books, *First Comes Love, Then Comes Money*, we told the story of the day Scott went to the big-box store to buy a new speaker for the TV setup in the basement. We'd agreed to spend about $500 on a speaker. So when Scott came home a few hours later with a car full of home theater equipment and a bill for nearly $5,000, it was all I could do to walk away and calm down before I said something I knew I'd regret.

Fortunately, Scott suffers from buyer's remorse—that's his Opposite Dynamic kicking in. So before I said a word about the equipment, he had already decided what he would return to the store. When I was finally cooled down enough to talk about the situation, Scott was the first one to offer a compromise. He said, "Look, we didn't really do enough research about speakers. It turns out that what we need is going to cost more than $500. But we don't need all of this. I'm willing to return all of it if that's what you want." That was a nice offer, but we still wanted a speaker, so together, we decided to return everything but a set of speakers. We ended up spending more than we'd planned, but we made the decision together.

So many of the couples we work with have forgotten how to compromise. But once you have learned about each other's Money Personalities, once you've started expressing your needs in your Money Huddles, once you've begun the repair work on your Money Relationship, finding a way forward that will satisfy both of you becomes a whole lot easier.

You're going to have conflict about money. One day, maybe soon, one of you is going to make a decision that drives the other one crazy. But if you *stop* and give yourself time to calm down, *drop* the assumptions and look for what's real, and *roll* up your sleeves and do the work to solve the problem, those conflicts will turn into opportunities to strengthen your Money Relationship.

MAKE IT HAPPEN

Each one of you share a story where you could have used Stop, Drop, and Roll to resolve a difficult situation.

A Million Dreams

You should be very proud of yourselves. You've done something amazing, something that will change your marriage for good. We know this stuff isn't always easy—sometimes it can be downright painful. But we also know that when couples commit to changing their patterns, when they join hands and move forward together, they can accomplish anything.

You might wrap up this book still deep in debt. You probably haven't made a big deposit on your retirement account over the last few weeks. Your financial picture might not be any better than it was when you started reading. But you know what? That's okay. Because you have made significant deposits in your relationship. You have made significant steps toward building a strong, healthy Money Relationship. And that's a lot more important than any budget or savings plan.

You've learned about your Money Personalities and

come to understand that each of us has our own way of thinking about and dealing with money. You've discovered that the Opposite Dynamic can create a sense of internal conflict when it comes to your personal money decisions, but you've also seen how your Opposite Dynamic can help you stay balanced and make smart money choices.

And you've learned about your spouse's Money Personality and how it connects and collides with yours. You've seen that when you play off of each other's strengths, you can conquer any money problem that comes up.

If you've had a history of financial infidelity in your relationship, we hope it's been brought to light and kicked to the curb. Of everything we've covered in this book, this might be the one thing that takes you a while to unpack, especially if you have years of secrets and hiding and lies to deal with. But you don't have to fix everything today. You have time and now you have a renewed sense of trust. We know that if you're both committed to transparency in all of your money decisions, it won't take long to repair the damage caused by financial infidelity.

You also have tools to take all of this knowledge and turn it into real action. Use your Money Dump to get everything out in the open, and then stick with your Money Huddles to keep the momentum going and plan your way back to your dreams.

When you find yourselves arguing about money, remember to Stop, Drop, and Roll to put out the flames of conflict and get yourselves cooled off. We know there will be times when you slip back into old patterns, but slipping doesn't mean you have to get stuck there. Stand up and try again. Soon, the new habits will become your new lifestyle.

Every marriage begins with a million dreams. And now you can get those dreams back. With every decision you make together, you will be one dream closer to the life you imagined on your wedding day.

The 5 Money Personalities Survival Guide

You know that in one way or another, money has an impact on every decision you make. That's why our Money Personalities play such an important role in our relationships. But there are a handful of big money moments in which our Money Personalities really get pumping—the holidays, birthdays, and vacations. These are the times our Money Personalities go into overdrive. And that can make already stressful situations even worse.

But when you understand your spouse's Money Personality, you can anticipate the stress points and work together to defuse a potential problem before it turns into an argument. You can see past the short temper or the anxiety or the efforts to control the situation and get to the heart of what's happening inside your spouse.

Here's what to expect from each of the five Money Personalities during some of the most stressful money moments in life. For a more extensive survival guide, head to TheMoneyCouple.com.

The Saver

We live in a culture of spending, and that's never as evident as it is during these money moments. That means the Saver is constantly surrounded by pressure to buy more, spend more, and give more. And that's stressful. The Saver will respond to this pressure by trying to control her spending and the spending of everyone in her family.

Here's how to help your Saver conquer the mountain of stress that comes from the big money moments:

HOLIDAYS. During the holidays, the Saver will complain about every purchase that comes in the house—the gifts, the food, the wrapping paper. She'll get downright Grinchy about the whole thing, and that adds to everyone's stress. But the nice thing about holidays is that you can plan for them. And that's what the Saver needs to do.

Well before a holiday arrives, sit down with your Saver and talk through your budget for the big day. Get as detailed as you can. Think about gifts, travel, and extra food for parties or visiting family. Then make a plan for setting aside the money you'll need before anyone spends a nickel. When a Saver knows there's money in the bank to cover holiday expenses, she can relax and enjoy the festivities.

BIRTHDAYS. Like other holidays, birthdays can bring out the worst in a Saver. And once again, planning ahead is a huge help. But you can also help your Saver manage the spending stress of birthdays by setting up clear expectations. Most Savers feel a lot better about a purchase when they know they are spending their money on something useful, something they know the person getting the gift will enjoy. Buying something for the sake of buying it feels like a waste of money for the Saver.

If your birthday is coming up, give your Saver spouse a few ideas for gifts you'd like. That gives her some options on price point but also lets her find something she's certain you'll appreciate.

VACATIONS. The Saver can be a major joy killer on vacation. Often, she can get so focused on how much things cost that she misses out on the fun of being together. When you and your Saver plan a vacation, make sure the budget includes not just hotel and travel expenses, but incidentals like taxi fares, tips, and tickets for events or the zoo or a show. And leave some room for spontaneous fun. Savers hate money surprises, so the more prepared she is for spending, the better.

If you can, plan for these money moments in advance to make sure you have some money set aside. The Saver is brilliant at finding ways to cut back in other areas to make room for spending in a different area. So start early and let the Saver do what she does best.

The Spender

No one loves a money moment more than a Spender. If you're married to a Spender, be prepared for the rush of adrenaline he feels when money moments come along. And be prepared for the anxiety and guilt Spenders can feel when they realize they've spent too much.

Here's how you can help your Spender keep an even keel during life's big money moments:

HOLIDAYS. Holidays are like Spender-palooza—it's the season for giving, and Spenders love to give. When the holidays arrive, don't be surprised if your Spender has started his shopping months in advance. He might even have a stash of gifts hidden in the back of some closet.

But money moments can be stressful for Spenders too. Spenders worry they'll run out of time to do all the shopping they hope to do. They get nervous about making sure they have just the right gift for everyone on their list. They can become obsessive about plans and details, running out at the last minute to replace all the silverware before the family arrives or grabbing one more last-minute gift the day before Christmas.

Like the Saver, the Spender will find holidays a lot more manageable if he has a clear budget. But unlike the Saver, the Spender needs this budget to release his sense of guilt and to keep him from ending up with too much debt when the bills come in.

BIRTHDAYS. Birthdays and anniversaries bring another chance for your Spender to shop for someone he loves. Again, the budget makes all the difference. But in this case, you might need to take the lead. Give your Spender spouse a ballpark figure for gifts and parties. You might say, "Honey, I know your brother's birthday is coming up. I think we can throw a great party for under $300." Without some parameters, the Spender will be overwhelmed by the possibilities. But most Spenders are willing to stick with a budget they had a hand in putting together, especially when they know they have their spouse's blessing to spend.

VACATIONS. Vacations are a Spender's paradise— so many purchases, so little time. And when you travel, remember that the Spender will be ready to drop a little cash on every souvenir, attraction, and $6 Diet Coke he can find. If there's a show in town, he'll want to see it. Some random attraction out by the interstate? He's there. And all of those little side trips and trinkets can add up fast.

Spenders worry they are missing out on a great experience if they don't see everything there is to see while on vacation, so once again, planning is everything. Do some research before you head out. Look at the options and plan out what you want to do and see; then make room in your budget for as much of it as you can. When your Spender knows he's not going to miss out on the good stuff, he'll relax and enjoy just being together.

The Security Seeker

The Security Seeker, like the Saver, can have a rough go of it during money moments. But for the Security Seeker, it's not about the amount of money that's spent. It's where that money will come from. The Security Seeker's main worry in life is that there won't be enough down the road. But few Security Seekers know what "enough" should be. They live with a kind of low-grade stress for most of their adult lives. That stress, however, spikes during money moments as they watch what they fear is their life savings getting thrown out at the mall.

Here's how you can help your Security Seeker relax:

HOLIDAYS. Security Seekers do best when they have a lot of input on the holiday budget. But unlike Savers who are hoping to spend as little as possible, Security Seekers can be fine with spending, as long as they know it's not going to make a dent in their future plans. That's why a well-defined budget is important, but not as important as a plan for making that budget work. As the holidays get closer, work with your Security Seeker spouse to figure out where you can cut back to afford some holiday splurges. Then as the big event gets closer, remind your spouse that you've worked hard—together—to make sure all of this fun is paid for.

BIRTHDAYS. Security Seekers aren't big fans of the splurge, but that doesn't mean they are reluctant gift givers. You can do a lot to ease your spouse's anxiety about birthdays by assuring him about the birthday plans.

VACATIONS. As you and your Security Seeker spouse plan your vacation, make sure you're both very clear about where this money will come from. Will you need to take on a little extra credit card debt to cover the expenses? Do you need to tap into your savings to pay for it? If you do, how can you adjust your budget to get that money back in place?

This can seem like a lot of work if you're not a Security Seeker, but a little effort on the front end of a vacation means a whole lot more enjoyment once you're there.

Security Seekers can seem unnecessarily anxious to the rest of us, but their fears come from the heart. They want to make sure their families are cared for down the road. So the last thing they need is a spouse who tells them to stop worrying. Instead, help your spouse focus on the present as well as the future. Remind her that the memories you make on vacation or during the holidays are an investment in the family too.

The Risk Taker

For Risk Takers, money moments are a time to get creative. So nothing makes a Risk Taker crabbier than being hemmed in by tradition. If you have a Risk Taker in your life, your biggest challenge will be to give him the leeway to be himself in the middle of what can often be already-chaotic situations.

Here's how to make the most of your Risk Taker's sense of adventure:

HOLIDAYS. Risk Takers love to think of new ways to celebrate the holidays. They're likely to suggest anything from having a Mexican feast for Christmas dinner to heading to Times Square for New Year's Eve. If you're married to a Risk Taker, be prepared to listen to some out-there ideas about gifts, food, travel, even holiday decorations. And when we say listen, we mean really listen.

If you're not a Risk Taker, it's easy to dismiss your spouse's ideas as ridiculous and impossible. But maybe there are a few ideas in there that would make life even more enjoyable for all of you. Is there really anything wrong with Christmas fajitas?

BIRTHDAYS. Having a spouse who's a Risk Taker can be pretty great when your birthday rolls around. Your spouse's sense of adventure means you never know what your celebration will involve. But if you worry that your spouse's spontaneity is going to get you both into financial hot water, be clear about these concerns well ahead of the actual event. The Risk Taker wants you to have a great time, and if she knows spending too much will keep you from enjoying yourself, she'll be more than happy to find a way to have a blast on a budget.

VACATIONS. For a Risk Taker, a vacation isn't really a vacation unless there's some thrill involved, whether it's a trip to an unknown location or a day of hang gliding once you get there. If your Risk Taker's ideas are going to break the bank, however, help her find ways to express her sense of adventure and creativity with more affordable options. What gets Risk Takers excited isn't how much something costs; it's the thrill of something new and different and unknown. And that doesn't have to cost anything. Challenge your Risk Taker to come up with inventive ideas on the cheap and she'll rise to the occasion.

The Flyer

Since Flyers rarely think about money, they don't get stressed out about money moments. But they do get anxious about all the planning that's part of the vacations or birthdays or holidays.

Here's how you can help your Flyer manage the stress of money moments:

HOLIDAYS. Because Flyers are not inclined to plan ahead, they are prone to last-minute impulse decisions—and that can lead to overspending and stress. So help your Flyer by talking about your holiday budget early. Make sure to give him plenty of input on the budget; it's easy to become controlling with a Flyer, but that just leads to resentment down the road.

Talk about what kinds of gifts you'd like to get for the people on your list. If you're having guests, figure out what you'll feed them and map out a plan for getting everything ready on time. Having all the details put together ahead of time means less last-minute impulse spending.

BIRTHDAYS. The Flyer is as likely to forget your birthday as she is to put together an over-the-top, thoughtful celebration. That means it helps to drop some helpful hints as you lead up to a birthday to remind your spouse that it really is the thought that counts.

VACATIONS. Flyers like to be fairly spontaneous, so be ready for your vacation plans to morph a bit as you get ready to travel. Flyers are also more than willing to make sure everyone on the vacation gets some say in how you will spend your time, so talk about your expectations for what to see and do and where to stay.

Because they tend to be spontaneous and fairly stress-free, Flyers can add a needed bit of fun and enjoyment to every money moment. They are great at being present in the moment and can help everyone around them do the same.